# THE
# HIGHWAY
# CODE

FOR NORTHERN IRELAND

Belfast: The Stationery Office

# Contents

# Introduction

*The Highway Code for Northern Ireland (hereafter referred to as the Highway Code)* is essential reading for everyone. Its rules apply to all road users: pedestrians, horse riders and cyclists, as well as motorcyclists and drivers.

Many of the rules in the Code are legal requirements, and if you disobey these rules you are committing a criminal offence. You may be fined, given penalty points on your licence or be disqualified from driving. In the most serious cases you may be sent to prison. Such rules are identified by the use of the words **MUST**/**MUST NOT**. In addition, each rule where appropriate, includes an abbreviated reference to the legislation which creates the offence. An explanation of the abbreviations is on pages 86 and 87.

Although failure to comply with the other rules of the Code will not, in itself, cause a person to be prosecuted, *The Highway Code* may be used in evidence in any court proceedings under the Traffic Legislation to establish liability.

Knowing and applying the rules contained in *The Highway Code* could significantly reduce road accident casualties. Cutting the number of deaths and injuries that occur on our roads every day is a responsibility we all share. *The Highway Code* can help us discharge that responsibility.

*The Highway Code* is based closely on the Great Britain version. Although Northern Ireland road safety legislation continues to be brought more into line with that of Great Britain, there are still some differences which it has been necessary to reflect in this issue. For example many Northern Ireland road users may not be familiar with toucan and puffin crossings or trams. References to these issues have however been included as some Northern Ireland residents visit Great Britain from time to time and might find the references helpful. It is recommended that anyone, especially drivers, intending to visit Great Britain should also purchase the Great Britain version of the *The Highway Code.*

# Rules for pedestrians

## General guidance

**1. Footways or footpaths** should be used if provided. Where possible, avoid walking next to the kerb with your back to the traffic. If you have to step into the road, look both ways first.

**2. If there is no footway or footpath,** walk on the right-hand side of the road so that you can see oncoming traffic. You should take extra care and
• be prepared to walk in single file, especially on narrow roads or in poor light
• keep close to the side of the road.
It may be safer to cross the road well before a sharp right-hand bend (so that oncoming traffic has a better chance of seeing you). Cross back after the bend.

**3. Help other road users to see you.** Wear or carry something light coloured, bright or fluorescent in poor daylight conditions. When it is dark, use reflective materials (e.g. armbands, sashes, waistcoats and jackets), which can be seen, by drivers using headlights, up to three times as far away as non-reflective materials.

Be seen in the dark; wear something reflective

**4. Young children** should not be out alone on the footpath, footway or road (see Rule 7). When taking children out, walk between them and the traffic and hold their hands firmly. Strap very young children in push-chairs or use reins.

5

**5. Organised walks.** Groups of people should use a footpath or footway if available; if one is not, they should keep to the left. Look-outs should be positioned at the front and back of the group, and they should wear fluorescent clothes in daylight and reflective clothes in the dark. At night, the look-out in front should carry a white light and the one at the back a red light. People on the outside of large groups should also carry lights and wear reflective clothing.

**6. Motorways.** You **MUST NOT** walk on motorways or slip roads except in an emergency (see Rule 249).
*Law RTRO Art 20 & MTR*

## Crossing the road

**7. The Green Cross Code.** The advice given below on crossing the road is for all pedestrians. Children should be taught the Code and should not be allowed out alone until they can understand and use it properly. The age when they can do this is different for each child. Many children cannot judge how fast vehicles are going or how far away they are. Children learn by example, so parents and carers should always use the Code in full when out with their children. They are responsible for deciding at what age children can use it safely by themselves.

**a. First find a safe place to cross.** It is safer to cross using a subway, a footbridge, an island, a zebra, pelican, toucan or puffin crossing, or where there is a crossing point controlled by a police officer, a school crossing patrol or a traffic warden. Where there is a crossing nearby, use it. Otherwise choose a place where you can see clearly in all directions. Try to avoid crossing between parked cars (see Rule 14) and on blind bends and brows of hills. Move to a space where drivers can see you clearly.

**b. Stop just before you get to the kerb,** where you can see if anything is coming. Do not get too close to the traffic. If there is no footpath or footway, keep back from the edge of the road but make sure you can still see approaching traffic.

**c. Look all around for traffic and listen.** Traffic could come from any direction. Listen as well, because you can sometimes hear traffic before you see it.

**d. If traffic is coming, let it pass.** Look all around again and listen. Do not cross until there is a safe gap in the traffic and you are certain that there is plenty of time. Remember, even if traffic is a long way off, it may be approaching very quickly.

**e. When it is safe, go straight across the road – do not run.** Keep looking and listening for traffic while you cross, in case there is any traffic you did not see, or in case other traffic appears suddenly.

**8. At a junction.** When crossing the road, look out for traffic turning into the road, especially from behind you.

**9. Pedestrian Safety Barriers.** Where there are barriers, cross the road only at the gaps provided for pedestrians. Do not climb over the barriers or walk between them and the road.

**10. Tactile paving.** Small raised studs which can be felt underfoot may be used to advise blind or partially sighted people that they are approaching a crossing point with a dropped kerb.

**11. One-way streets.** Check which way the traffic is moving. Do not cross until it is safe to do so without stopping. Bus and cycle lanes may operate in the opposite direction to the rest of the traffic.

**12. Bus and cycle lanes.** Take care when crossing these lanes as traffic may be moving faster than in the other lanes, or against the flow of traffic.

**13. Routes shared with cyclists.** Cycle tracks may run alongside footpaths, with a dividing line segregating the two. Keep to the section for pedestrians. Take extra care where cyclists and pedestrians share the same path without separation (see Rule 48).

**14. Parked vehicles.** If you have to cross between parked vehicles, use the outside edges of the vehicles as if they were the kerb. Stop there and make sure you can see all around and that the traffic can see you. Never cross the road in front of, or behind, any vehicle with its engine running, especially a large vehicle, as the driver may not be able to see you.

**15. Reversing vehicles.** Never cross behind a vehicle which is reversing, showing white reversing lights or sounding a warning.

**16. Moving vehicles.** You **MUST NOT** get on to or hold on to a moving vehicle.
*Law RTO 1995 Art 37*

**17. At night.** Wear something reflective to make it easier for others to see you (see Rule 3). If there is no pedestrian crossing nearby, cross the road near a street light so that traffic can see you more easily.

## Crossings
**18. At all crossings.** When using any type of crossing you should
- always check that the traffic has stopped before you start to cross or push a pram onto a crossing
- always cross between the studs or over the zebra markings. Do not cross at the side of the crossing or on the zigzag lines, as it can be dangerous.

You **MUST NOT** loiter on zebra, pelican or puffin crossings.
*Laws PPCR, ZPCR & RTRO Art 59*

**19. Zebra crossings.** Give traffic plenty of time to see you and to stop before you start to cross. Vehicles will need more time when the road is slippery. Remember that traffic does not have to stop until someone has moved onto the crossing. Wait until traffic has stopped from both directions or the road is clear before crossing. Keep looking both ways, and listening, in case a driver or rider has not seen you and attempts to overtake a vehicle that has stopped.

**20.** Where there is an island in the middle of a zebra crossing, wait on the island and follow Rule 19 before you cross the second half of the road – it is a separate crossing.

**21. At traffic lights.** There may be special signals for pedestrians. You should only start to cross the road when the green figure shows. If you have started to cross the road and the green figure goes out, you should still have time to reach the other side, but do not delay. If no pedestrian signals have been provided, watch carefully and do not cross until the traffic lights are red and the traffic has stopped. Keep looking and check for traffic that may be turning the corner. Remember that traffic lights may let traffic move in some lanes while traffic in other lanes has stopped.

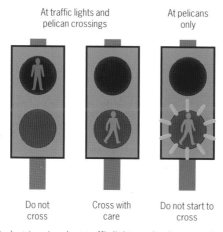

At traffic lights and
pelican crossings

At pelicans
only

Do not
cross

Cross with
care

Do not start to
cross

Pedestrian signals at traffic lights and pelican crossings

**22. Pelican crossings.** These are signal-controlled crossings operated by pedestrians. Push the control button to activate the traffic signals. When the red figure shows, do not cross. When a steady green figure shows, check that traffic has stopped then cross with care. When the green figure begins to flash you should not start to cross. If you have already started you should have time to finish crossing safely.

**23.** At some pelican crossings there is a bleeping sound to indicate to blind or partially-sighted people when the steady green figure is showing, and there may be a tactile signal to help deafblind people.

**24.** When the road is congested, traffic on your side of the road may be forced to stop even though their lights are green. Traffic may still be moving on the other side of the road, so press the button and wait for the signal to cross.

**25. Puffin and toucan crossings.** These differ from pelican crossings as there is no flashing green figure phase. On puffin crossings the red and green figures are above the control box on your side of the road. Press the button and wait for the green figure to show. On toucan crossings cyclists are permitted to ride across the road (see Rule 65).

**26. 'Staggered' pelican or puffin crossings.** When the crossings on each side of the central refuge are not in line they are two separate crossings. On reaching the central island press the button again and wait for a steady green figure.

**27. Crossings controlled by an authorised person.** Do not cross the road unless you are signalled to do so by a police officer, traffic warden or school crossing patrol. Always cross in front of them.

**28.** Where there are no controlled crossing points available it is advisable to cross where there is an island in the middle of the road. Use the Green Cross Code to cross to the island and then stop and use it again to cross the second half of the road.

## Situations needing extra care

**29. Emergency vehicles.** If an ambulance, fire engine, police or other emergency vehicle approaches using flashing blue lights, headlights and/or sirens, keep off the road.

**30. Buses.** Get on or off a bus only when it has stopped to allow you to do so. Watch out for cyclists when you are getting off. Never cross the road directly behind or in front of a bus; wait until it has moved off and you can see the road clearly in both directions.

**31. Tramways.** These may run through pedestrian areas. Their path will be marked out by shallow kerbs, changes in the paving or other road surface, white lines or yellow dots. Cross at designated crossings where provided. Flashing amber lights may warn you that a tram is approaching. Elsewhere look both ways along the track before crossing. Do not walk along the track. Trams move quickly and silently and cannot steer to avoid you.

**32. Railway level crossings.** Do not cross if the red lights show, an alarm is sounding or the barriers are being lowered.

The tone of the alarm will change if another train is approaching. If there are no lights, alarms or barriers, stop, look both ways and listen before crossing.

**33. Street footpath and footway repairs.** A footpath or footway may be closed temporarily because it is not safe to use. Take extra care if you are directed to walk in or to cross the road.

# Rules about animals

## Horseriders

**34. Safety equipment.** Children under the age of 14 MUST wear a helmet which complies with the Regulations. It MUST be fastened securely. Other riders should also follow this advice.
*Law H(PHYR)O Art 3 & H(PHYR)R*

**35. Other clothing.** You should wear
- boots or shoes with hard soles and heels
- light coloured or fluorescent clothing in daylight
- reflective clothing if you have to ride at night or in poor visibility.

**36. At night.** It is safer not to ride on the road at night or in poor visibility, but if you do, make sure your horse has reflective bands above the fetlock joints. Carry lights which show white to the front and red to the rear.

## Riding
**37.** Before you take a horse on to a road, you should
- ensure all tack fits well and is in good condition
- make sure you can control the horse.
Always ride with other, less nervous horses if you think that your horse will be nervous of traffic. Never ride a horse without a saddle or bridle.

**38.** Before riding off or turning, look behind you to make sure it is safe, then give a clear arm signal.

**39.** When riding on the road you should
- keep to the left
- keep both hands on the reins unless you are signalling
- keep both feet in the stirrups
- not carry another person
- not carry anything which might affect your balance or get tangled up with the reins
- keep a horse you are leading to your left
- move in the direction of the traffic flow in a one-way street
- never ride more than two abreast, and ride in single file where the road narrows or on the approach to a bend.

**40.** You should not take a horse on to a footpath, footway or cycle track.

**41.** Avoid roundabouts wherever possible. If you use them you should
- keep to the left and watch out for vehicles crossing your path to leave or join the roundabout
- signal right when riding across exits to show you are not leaving
- signal left just before you leave the roundabout.

## Other animals

**42. Dogs.** Do not let a dog out on the road on its own. Keep it on a short lead when walking on the footpath, footway, road or path shared with cyclists.

**43.** When in a vehicle make sure dogs or other animals are suitably restrained so they cannot distract you while you are driving or injure you if you stop quickly.

**44. Animals being herded.** These should be kept under control at all times. You should, if possible, send another person along the road in front to warn other road users, especially at a bend or the brow of a hill. It is safer not to move animals after dark, but if you do, then wear reflective clothing and ensure that lights are carried (white at the front and red at the rear of the herd).

# Rules for cyclists

These rules are in addition to those in the following sections, which apply to all vehicles (except the motorway section on page 58). See also page 82 on choosing and maintaining your bicycle.

**45. Clothing.** You should wear
- a cycle helmet which conforms to current regulations
- appropriate clothes for cycling. Avoid clothes which may get tangled in the chain, or in a wheel or may obscure your lights
- light-coloured or fluorescent clothing which helps other road users to see you in daylight and poor light
- reflective clothing and/or accessories (belt, arm or ankle bands) in the dark.

Help yourself to be seen

**46. Between sunset and sunrise** your cycle **MUST** have front and rear lights lit. It **MUST** also be fitted with a red rear reflector (and amber pedal reflectors, if manufactured after 24/1/96). White front reflectors and spoke reflectors will also help you to be seen.
*Law RVLR regs 21 & 27*

Any bicyle used on a public road **MUST** also have a working bell or horn fitted and effective front and rear brakes.
*Law RV (T)R*

## When cycling
**47.** Use cycle routes when practicable. They can make your journey safer.

**48. Cycle Tracks.** These are normally located away from the road, but may occasionally be found alongside footpaths or footways. Cyclists and pedestrians may be segregated or they may share the same space (unsegregated). When using segregated tracks you should keep to the side intended for cyclists. Take care when passing pedestrians, especially children, elderly or disabled people, and allow them plenty of room. Always be prepared to slow down and stop if necessary.

**49. Cycle Lanes.** These are marked by a white line (which may be broken) along the carriageway (see Rule 119). Keep within the lane wherever possible.

**50.** You **MUST** obey all traffic signs and traffic light signals.
*Laws RTO 1995 Art 50, TSR Reg 8*

**51.** You should
- keep both hands on the handlebars except when signalling or changing gear
- keep both feet on the pedals
- not ride more than two abreast
- ride in single file on narrow or busy roads
- not ride close behind another vehicle
- not carry anything which will affect your balance or may get tangled up with your wheels or chain
- be considerate of other road users, particularly blind and partially sighted pedestrians. Let them know you are there when necessary, for example, by sounding your bell or horn.

**52.** You should
- look all around before moving away from the kerb, turning or manoeuvring, to make sure it is safe to do so. Give a clear signal to show other road users what you intend to do (see page 71)
- look well ahead for obstructions in the road, such as drains, potholes and parked vehicles so that you do not have to swerve suddenly to avoid them. Leave plenty of room when passing parked vehicles and watch out for doors being opened into your path
- take extra care near road humps, narrowings and other traffic calming features.

**53.** You **MUST NOT**
- cycle on a footpath or footway unless on a cycle track where one has been provided
- carry a passenger unless your cycle has been built or adapted

to carry one
- hold on to a moving vehicle or trailer
- ride in a dangerous, careless or inconsiderate manner
- ride when under the influence of drink or drugs.

*Law RTO 1995 Arts 35, 37, 42, 43 & 44 RTRO Art 3*

**54.** You should not leave your cycle where it would endanger or obstruct other road users or pedestrians, for example, lying on the footpath or footway. Use cycle parking facilities where provided.

**55.** You MUST NOT cross the stop line when the traffic lights are red. Some junctions have an advanced stop line to enable you to position yourself ahead of other traffic (see Rule 154).

*Law TSR reg 33(1)*

**56. Bus Lanes.** These may be used by cyclists only if the signs include a cycle symbol. Watch out for people getting on or off a bus. Be very careful when overtaking a bus or leaving a bus lane as you will be entering a busier traffic flow.

## Road junctions
**57. On the left.** When approaching a junction on the left, watch out for vehicles turning in front of you, out of or into the side road. Do not ride on the inside of vehicles signalling or slowing down to turn left.

**58.** Pay particular attention to long vehicles which need a lot of room to manoeuvre at corners. They may have to move over to the right before turning left. Wait until they have completed the manoeuvre because the rear wheels come very close to the kerb while turning. Do not be tempted to ride in the space between them and the kerb.

**59. On the right.** If you are turning right, check the traffic to ensure it is safe, then signal and move to the centre of the road. Wait until there is a safe gap in the oncoming traffic before completing the turn. It may be safer to wait on the left until there is a safe gap or to dismount and push your cycle across the road.

**60. Dual carriageways.** Remember that traffic on most dual carriageways moves quickly. When crossing wait for a safe gap and cross each carriageway in turn. Take extra care when crossing slip roads.

## Roundabouts

**61.** Full details about the correct procedure at roundabouts are contained in Rules 160–166. Roundabouts can be hazardous and should be approached with care.

**62.** You may feel safer either keeping to the left on the roundabout or dismounting and walking your cycle round on the footpath, footway or verge. If you decide to keep to the left you should

- be aware that drivers may not easily see you
- take extra care when cycling across exits and you may need to signal right to show you are not leaving the roundabout
- watch out for vehicles crossing your path to leave or join the roundabout.

**63.** Give plenty of room to long vehicles on the roundabout as they need more space to manoeuvre. Do not ride in the space they need to get round the roundabout. It may be safer to wait until they have cleared the roundabout.

## Crossing the road

**64.** Do not ride across a pelican, puffin or zebra crossing. Dismount and wheel your cycle across.

**65. Toucan crossings.** These are light-controlled crossings which allow cyclists and pedestrians to cross at the same time. They are push button operated. Pedestrians and cyclists will see the green signal together. Cyclists are permitted to ride across.

**66. Cycle-only crossings.** Cycle tracks on opposite sides of the road may be linked by signalled crossings. You may ride across but you **MUST NOT** cross until the green cycle symbol is showing.

*Law TSR reg 33(1)*

# Rules for motorcyclists

These Rules are in addition to those in all following sections which apply to all vehicles. For motorcycle licence requirements see page 83.

## General

**67.** On all journeys, the rider and pillion passenger on a motorcycle, scooter or moped **MUST** wear a protective helmet. Helmets **MUST** comply with the Regulations and they **MUST** be fastened securely. It is also advisable to wear eye protection, which **MUST** comply with the Regulations. Consider wearing ear protection.  Strong boots, gloves and suitable clothing may help to protect you if you fall off.
*Laws MC(PH)R (as amended) reg2, RTO 1995 Arts 27 & 28, MC(EP)R(as amended)reg2 & RTO 1995 Art 29*

**68.** You **MUST NOT** carry more than one pillion passenger and he/she **MUST** sit astride the machine on a proper seat and should keep both feet on the footrests.
*Laws MC(PH)R & RTO 1995 Art 34*

**69. Daylight riding.** Make yourself as visible as possible from the side as well as the front and rear. You could wear a white or brightly coloured helmet. Wear  fluorescent clothing or strips. Dipped headlights, even in good daylight, may also make you more conspicuous.

Make sure you can be seen

**70. Riding in the dark.** Wear reflective clothing or strips, to improve your chances of being seen in the dark. These reflect light from the headlamps of other vehicles making you more visible from a long distance. See Rules 93–96 for lighting requirements.

**71. Manoeuvring.** You should be aware of what is behind and to the sides before manoeuvring. Look behind you; use mirrors if they are fitted. When overtaking traffic queues look out for pedestrians crossing between vehicles and vehicles emerging from junctions.
**Remember: Observation – Signal – Manoeuvre.**

# Rules for drivers and motorcyclists

**72. Vehicle condition.** You **MUST** ensure your vehicle and trailer complies with the full requirements of the Motor Vehicles (Construction and Use) Regulations (NI) and the Road Vehicles Lighting Regulations (NI). (See page 89 and 90).

**73. Before setting off.** You should ensure that
- you have planned your route and allowed sufficient time
- clothing and footwear do not prevent you using the controls in the correct manner
- you know where all the controls are and how to use them before you need them. All vehicles are different; do not wait until it is too late to find out
- your mirrors and seat are adjusted correctly to ensure comfort, full control and maximum vision
- head restraints are properly adjusted to reduce the risk of neck injuries in the event of an accident
- you have sufficient fuel before commencing your journey, especially if it includes motorway driving. It can be dangerous to lose power when driving in traffic.

## 74. Vehicle towing and loading. As a driver

- you **MUST NOT** tow more than your licence permits you to
- you **MUST NOT** overload your vehicle or trailer. You should not tow a weight greater than that recommended by the manufacturer of your vehicle
- you **MUST** secure your load and it **MUST NOT** stick out dangerously
- you should properly distribute the weight in your caravan or trailer, with heavy items mainly over the axle(s) and ensure a downward load on the tow ball. Manufacturer's recommended weight and tow ball load should not be exceeded. This should avoid the possibility of swerving or snaking and going out of control. If this does happen, ease off the accelerator and reduce speed gently to regain control.

*Laws CUR reg 115 & MV(DL)R reg 32*

## Seat Belts

**75.** You **MUST** wear a seat belt if one is available, unless you are exempt. Those exempt from the requirement include the holders of medical exemption certificates and people making local deliveries in a vehicle designed for the purpose.

*Laws RTO 1995 Arts 23 & 24, MV(WSB)R & MV(WSBFS)R*

## Seat belt requirements

This table summarises the main legal requirements for wearing seat belts in Cars, Light Goods Vehicles and small Buses

| | FRONT SEAT (all vehicles) | REAR SEAT (cars and small minibuses*) | WHOSE RESPONSIBILITY |
|---|---|---|---|
| **DRIVER** | **MUST** be worn if fitted | | **DRIVER** |
| **CHILD** under 3 years of age | Appropriate child restraint **MUST** be worn | Appropriate child restraint **MUST** be worn *if available* | **DRIVER** |
| **CHILD** aged 3 to 11 and under 1.5metres (about 5 feet) in height | Appropriate child restraint **MUST** be worn *if available.* If not, an adult seat belt **MUST** be worn | Appropriate child restraint **MUST** be worn *if available* If not, an adult seat belt **MUST** be worn *if available.* | **DRIVER** |
| **CHILD** aged 12 or 13 or younger child 1.5 metres or more in height | Adult seat belt **MUST** be worn *if available.* | Adult seat belt **MUST** be worn *if available* | **DRIVER** |
| **PASSENGER** over the age of 14 | **MUST** be worn *if available* | **MUST** be worn *if available* | **PASSENGER** |

\* Minibuses with an unladen weight of 2540kg or less

**76.** The driver **MUST** ensure that all children under 14 years of age wear seat belts or sit in an appropriate child restraint. This means a baby seat, child seat, booster seat or booster cushion appropriate to the child's weight and size, fitted to the manufacturer's instructions.

*Laws RTO 1995 Arts 23 & 24, MV(WSB)R & MV(WSBCFS)R*

Make sure children wear the correct restraint

**77.** You **MUST** wear seatbelts in minibuses with an unladen weight of up to 2540 kg or less. You should wear them in large minibuses, buses and coaches where available.

*Laws RTO 1995 Arts 23 & 24, MV(WSB)R & MV(WSBCFS)R*

**78. Children in cars.** Drivers who are carrying children in cars should ensure that

- children do not sit behind the rear seats in an estate car or hatchback, unless a special child seat has been fitted
- the child safety door locks, where fitted, are used when children are in the car
- children are kept under control
- a rear-facing baby seat is **NEVER** fitted into a seat protected by an airbag.

## Fitness to drive
**79. Make sure that you are fit to drive.** You **MUST** report to Driver and Vehicle Licensing Northern Ireland (DVLNI) any health condition likely to affect your driving.

*Law RTO 1981 Art 11*

**80.** Driving when you are tired greatly increases your accident risk. To minimise this risk

- make sure you are fit to drive. Do not undertake a long journey (longer than an hour) if you feel tired
- avoid undertaking long journeys between midnight and 6am, when natural alertness is at a minimum

- plan your journey to take sufficient breaks. A minimum break of at least 15 minutes after every two hours of driving is recommended
- if you feel at all sleepy, stop in a safe place. Do not stop on the hard shoulder of a motorway
- the most effective ways to counter sleepiness are to take a short nap (up to 15 minutes) or drink, for example, two cups of strong coffee. Fresh air, exercise or turning up the radio may help for a short time, but are ***not*** as effective.

**81. Vision.** You **MUST** be able to read a vehicle number plate from a distance of 20.5 metres (67 feet – about five car lengths) in good daylight. You **MUST** be able to read a new style number plate from a distance of 20 metres (66 feet). If you need to wear glasses (or contact lenses) to do this, you **MUST** wear them at all times whilst driving. The police have the power to require a driver, at any time, to undertake an eyesight test in good daylight.

*Laws RTO 1981 Art 154 & MV(DL)R reg 29 & Sch 7, MVDL(A) & MC(DI)(A)R*

**82.** At night or in poor visibility, do not use tinted glasses, lenses or visors or anything that restricts vision.

## Alcohol and drugs

**83. Do not drink and drive** as it will seriously affect your judgement and abilities. You **MUST NOT** drive with a breath alcohol level higher than 35 µg /100ml or a blood alcohol level of more than 80 mg/100 ml. Alcohol will

- give a false sense of confidence
- reduce co-ordination and slow down reactions
- affect judgement of speed, distance and risk
- reduce your driving ability, even if you are below the legal limit
- take time to leave your body; you may be unfit to drive in the evening after drinking at lunchtime, or in the morning after drinking the previous evening. If you are going to drink, arrange another means of transport.

*Law RTO 1995 Arts 13, 15 & 16*

**84.** You **MUST NOT** drive under the influence of drugs or medicine. Check the instructions or ask your doctor or pharmacist. Using illegal drugs is highly dangerous. Never take them before driving; the effects are unpredictable, can be even more severe than alcohol and may result in fatal or serious road accidents.

*Law RTO 1995 Art 15*

# General rules, techniques and advice for all drivers and riders

This section should be read by all drivers, motorcyclists and cyclists. The rules in *The Highway Code* do not give you the right of way in any circumstance, but they advise you when you should give way to others. Always give way if it can help to avoid an accident.

## Signals

**85.** Signals warn and inform other road users, including pedestrians (see page 71), of your intended actions.
You should

- give clear signals in plenty of time, having checked it is not misleading to signal at that time
- use them, if necessary, before changing course or direction, stopping or moving off
- cancel them after use
- make sure your signals will not confuse others. If, for instance , you want to stop after a side road, do not signal until you are passing the road. If you signal earlier it may give the impression that you intend to turn into the road. Your brake lights will warn traffic behind you that you are slowing down
- use an arm signal to emphasise or reinforce your signal if necessary. Remember that signalling does not give you priority.

**86.** You should also

- watch out for signals given by other road users and proceed only when you are satisfied that it is safe
- be aware that an indicator on another vehicle may not have been cancelled.

**87.** You **MUST** obey signals given by police officers and traffic wardens (see page 72) and signs used by school crossing patrols.

*Laws RTRO Art 60, RTO 1995 Art 49 & RT(TW)O Art 2*

## Traffic light signals and traffic signs

**88.** You **MUST** obey all traffic light signals (see page 70) and traffic signs giving orders, including temporary signals and signs (see pages 73 and 78) . Make sure you know, understand and act on all other traffic and information signs and road markings (see pages 74 – 80).
*Law RTO Art 49 & TSR regs 8, 13, 14, 24, 25, 26 & 33*

**89. Police stopping procedures.** If the police want to stop your vehicle they will, where possible, attract your attention by
- flashing blue lights or headlights or sounding their siren or horn
- directing you to pull over to the side by pointing and/or using the left indicator.

You **MUST** then pull over and stop as soon as it is safe to do so. Then switch off your engine.
*Law RTO 1981 Art 180*

**90. Flashing headlights.** Only flash your headlights to let other road users know that you are there. Do not flash your headlights in an attempt to intimidate other road users.

**91.** If another driver flashes his headlights never assume that it is a signal to go. Use your own judgement and proceed carefully.

**92. The horn.** Use only while your vehicle is moving and you need to warn other road users of your presence. Never sound your horn aggressively. You **MUST NOT** use your horn
- while stationary on the road
- when driving in a built-up area between the hours of 11.30 pm and 7.00 am

***except*** when another vehicle poses a danger.
*Law CUR reg 114*

# Lighting requirements

**93.** You **MUST**
- use headlights during the hours of darkness (between half an hour after sunset and half an hour before sunrise)
- use headlights when visibility is seriously reduced (see Rule 201).
- ensure all sidelights and rear registration plate lights are lit between sunset and sunrise.

*Laws RVLR regs 27 & 28 & RV (DRM)R reg 9*

**94.** You **MUST NOT**
- use any lights in a way which would dazzle or cause discomfort to other road users
- use front or rear fog lights unless visibility is seriously reduced. You **MUST** switch them off when visibility improves to avoid dazzling other road users.

*Law RVLR reg 30*

**95.** You should also
- use dipped headlights in dull daytime weather, to ensure that you can be seen
- keep your headlights dipped when overtaking until you are level with the other vehicle and then change to main beam if necessary, unless this would dazzle oncoming traffic
- slow down, and if necessary stop, if you are dazzled by oncoming headlights.

**96. Hazard warning lights.** These may be used when your vehicle is stationary, to warn that it is temporarily obstructing traffic. Never use them as an excuse for dangerous or illegal parking. You **MUST NOT** use hazard warning lights whilst driving unless you are on a motorway or unrestricted dual carriageway and you need to warn drivers behind you of a hazard or obstruction ahead. Only use them for long enough to ensure that your warning has been observed.

*Law RVLR reg 30*

# Control of the vehicle

## Braking
**97. In normal circumstances.** The safest way to brake is to do so early and lightly. Brake more firmly as you begin to stop. Ease the pressure off just before the vehicle comes to rest to avoid a jerky stop.

**98. In an emergency.** Brake immediately. Try to avoid braking so harshly that you lock your wheels. Locked wheels can lead to skidding.

**99. Skids.** Skidding is caused by the driver braking, accelerating or steering too harshly or driving too fast for the road conditions. If skidding occurs, ease off the brake or accelerator and try to steer smoothly in the direction of the skid. For example, if the rear of the vehicle skids to the right, steer quickly and smoothly to the right to recover.

Rear of car skids          Driver steers
to the right               to the right

**100. ABS.** The presence of an anti-lock braking system should not cause you to alter the way you brake from that indicated in Rule 97. However in the case of an emergency, apply the footbrake rapidly and firmly; do not release the pressure until the vehicle has slowed to the desired speed. The ABS should ensure that steering control will be retained.

**101. Brakes affected by water.** If you have driven through deep water your brakes may be less effective. Test them at the first safe opportunity by pushing gently on the brake pedal to make sure that they work. If they are not fully effective, gently apply light pressure while driving slowly. This will help to dry them out.

**102. Coasting.** This term describes a vehicle travelling in neutral or with the clutch pressed down. Do not coast, whatever the driving conditions. It reduces driver control because

• engine braking is eliminated
• vehicle speed downhill will increase quickly
• increased use of the footbrake can reduce its effectiveness
• steering response will be affected particularly on bends and corners
• it may be more difficult to select the appropriate gear when needed.

The vehicle is also less likely to be heard by other road users.

## Speed limits
**103.** You **MUST NOT** exceed the maximum speed limits for the road and for your vehicle (see the table on page 26). Street lights usually mean that there is a 30 mph speed limit unless there are signs showing another limit.

*Law RTRO Arts 36, 39 & 43 & MV(SL)R*

# Speed Limits

| Type of vehicle | Built-up areas* | Elsewhere | | Motorways |
| | | Single carriage-ways | Dual carriage-ways | |
| | MPH | MPH | MPH | MPH |
|---|---|---|---|---|
| **Cars & motorcycles** (including car derived vans up to 2 tonnes maximum laden weight) | 30 | 60 | 70 | 70 |
| **Cars towing caravans or trailers** (including car derived vans and motorcycles) | 30 | 50 | 60 | 60 |
| **Buses & coaches** (not exceeding 12 metres in overall length) | 30 | 50 | 60 | 70 |
| **Goods vehicles** (not exceeding 7.5 tonnes maximum laden weight) | 30 | 50 | 60 | 70† |
| **Goods vehicles** (exceeding 7.5 tonnes maximum laden weight) | 30 | 40 | 50 | 60 |

These are the national speed limits and apply to all roads unless signs show otherwise.

*The 30 mph limit usually applies to all traffic on all roads where street lights are not more than 185 metres apart unless signs show otherwise.

†60 if articulated or towing a trailer

**104.** The speed limit is the absolute maximum and does not mean it is safe to drive at that speed irrespective of conditions. Driving at speeds too fast for the road and traffic conditions can be dangerous. You should always reduce your speed when

- the road layout or condition presents hazards, such as bends
- sharing the road with pedestrians and cyclists, particularly children, and motorcyclists
- weather conditions make it safer to do so
- driving at night as it is harder to see other road users.

## Stopping distances

**105.** Drive at a speed that will allow you to stop well within the distance you can see to be clear. You should

- leave enough space between you and the vehicle in front so that you can pull up safely if it suddenly slows down or stops. The safe rule is never to get closer than the overall stopping distance (see Typical Stopping Distances diagram, pages 28 – 29)
- allow at least a two second gap between you and the vehicle in front on roads carrying fast traffic. The gap should be at least doubled on wet roads and increased still further on icy roads
- remember, large vehicles and motorcycles need a greater distance to stop.

Use a fixed point to help measure a two second gap

# Typical Stopping Distances

20 mph  6 metres  6 metres
= 12 metres
(40 feet)
or 3 car lengths

30 mph  9 metres  14 metres
= 23 metres
(75 feet)
or 6 car lengths

40 mph  12 metres  24 metres
= 36 metres
(120 feet)
or 9 car lengths

50 mph  15 metres  38 metres

60 mph  18 metres  55 metres

70 mph  21 metres  75 metres

## Lines and lane markings on the road

Diagrams of all lines are shown on page 78.

**106. A broken white line.** This marks the centre of the road. When this line lengthens and the gaps shorten, it means that there is a hazard ahead. Do not cross it unless you can see the road is clear well ahead and wish to overtake or turn off.

**107. Double white lines where the line nearest to you is broken.** This means you may cross the lines to overtake if it is safe, provided you can complete the manoeuvre before reaching a solid white line on your side. White arrows on the road indicate when you need to get back onto your side of the road.

**108. Double white lines where the line nearest you is solid.** This means you **MUST NOT** cross or straddle it unless it is safe and you need to enter adjoining premises or a side road. You may cross the line if necessary to pass a stationary vehicle, or overtake a pedal cycle, horse or road maintenance vehicle, if they are travelling at 10mph or less.
*Law TSR reg 25*

**109. Areas of white diagonal stripes** or chevrons painted on the road. These are to separate traffic lanes or to protect traffic turning right.

Thinking Distance

Braking Distance

average car length = 4 metres

53 metres
75 feet)
13 car lengths

= 73 metres
(240 feet)
or 18 car lengths

= 96 metres
(315 feet)
or 24 car lengths

- If the area is bordered by a solid white line, you should not enter it except in an emergency.
- If the area is bordered by a broken white line, you should not enter the area unless it is necessary and you can see that it is safe to do so.
- If the area is on a motorway and consists of a triangle bounded by continuous white lines marked by chevrons, you **MUST NOT** enter it except in an emergency.

*Law TSR reg 25*

**110. Lane dividers.** These are short broken white lines which are used on wide carriageways to divide them into lanes. You should keep between them.

**111. Reflective road studs** may be used with white lines.

- White studs mark the lanes or the middle of the road.
- Red studs mark the left edge of the road.
- Amber studs mark the central reservation of a dual carriageway or motorway.

- Green studs mark the edge of the main carriageway at lay-bys, side roads and slip roads.

# Multi-lane carriageways

## Lane discipline

**112.** If you need to change lane, first use your mirrors and check your blind spots (the areas you are unable to see in the mirrors) to make sure you will not force another driver or rider to swerve or slow down. When it is safe to do so, signal to indicate your intentions to other road users and when clear move over.

**113.** You should follow the signs and road markings and get into lane as directed. In congested road conditions do not switch lanes unnecessarily.

## Single carriageway

**114.** Where a single carriageway has three lanes and the road markings or signs do not give priority to traffic in either direction

- use the middle lane only for overtaking or turning right. Remember, you have no more right to use the middle lane than a driver coming from the opposite direction
- do not use the right-hand lane.

**115.** Where a single carriageway has four or more lanes, use only the lanes that signs or markings indicate.

## Dual carriageways

**116.** On a two-lane dual carriageway you should stay in the left-hand lane. Use the right-hand lane for overtaking or turning right. If you use it for overtaking move back to the left-hand lane when it is safe to do so.

**117.** On a three-lane dual carriageway, you may use the middle lane or the right-hand lane to overtake but return to the middle and then the left-hand lane when it is safe.

**118. Climbing and crawler lanes.** These are provided on some hills. Use this lane if you are driving a slow moving vehicle or if there are vehicles behind you wishing to overtake.

**119. Cycle lanes.** These are shown by road markings and signs. You **MUST NOT** drive or park in a cycle lane marked by a solid white line during its times of operation. Do not drive or park in a cycle lane marked by a broken white line unless it is

unavoidable. You **MUST NOT** park in any cycle lane whilst waiting restrictions apply.
*Law RTRO Art 4(5)*

**120. Bus and tram lanes.** These are shown by road markings and signs. You **MUST NOT** drive or stop in a tram lane or in a bus lane during its period of operation unless the signs indicate you may do so.
*Law TSR reg 21*

**121. One-way streets.** Traffic **MUST** travel in the direction indicated by signs. Buses and/or cycles may have a contraflow lane. Choose the correct lane for your exit as soon as you can. Do not change lanes suddenly. Unless road signs or markings indicate otherwise, you should use
- the left-hand lane when going left
- the right-hand lane when going right
- the most appropriate lane when going straight ahead.
Remember – traffic could be passing on both sides.
*Laws RTO 1995 Art 50, RTRO Arts 4(5) & 5(9)*

# General advice

**122.** You **MUST NOT**
- drive dangerously
- drive without due care and attention
- drive without reasonable consideration for other road users.
*Laws RTO 1995 Arts 10 & 12*

**123.** You **MUST NOT** drive on or over a footpath or footway except to gain lawful access to property.
*Law RTRO 1997*

**124. Adapt your driving** to the appropriate type and condition of road you are on. In particular
- do not treat speed limits as a target. It is often not appropriate or safe to drive at the maximum speed limit
- take the road and traffic conditions into account. Be prepared for unexpected or difficult situations, for example, the road being blocked beyond a blind bend. Be prepared to adjust your speed as a precaution
- where there are junctions, be prepared for vehicles emerging
- in side roads and country lanes look out for unmarked junctions where nobody has priority

- try to anticipate what pedestrians and cyclists might do. If pedestrians, particularly children, are looking the other way, they may step out into the road without seeing you.

**125. Be considerate.** Be careful of and considerate towards other road users. You should
- try to be understanding if other drivers cause problems; they may be inexperienced or not know the area well
- be patient; remember that anyone can make a mistake
- not allow yourself to become agitated or involved if someone is behaving badly on the road. This will only make the situation worse. Pull over, calm down and, when you feel relaxed, continue your journey
- slow down and hold back if a vehicle pulls out into your path at a junction. Allow it to get clear. Do not over-react by driving too close behind it.

**126. Safe driving needs concentration.** Avoid distractions when driving such as
- loud music (this may mask other sounds)
- trying to read maps
- inserting a cassette or CD or tuning a radio
- arguing with your passengers or other road users
- eating and drinking.

## Mobile phones and in-car technology
**127.** You **MUST** exercise proper control of your vehicle at all times. Never use a hand held mobile phone or microphone when driving. Using hands free equipment is also likely to distract your attention from the road. It is far safer not to use any telephone while you are driving – find a safe place to stop first.
*Laws RTO 1995 Arts 10 & 12 & CUR reg 120*

**128.** There is a danger of driver distraction being caused by in-vehicle systems such as route guidance and navigation systems, congestion warning systems, PCs, multi-media, etc. Do not operate, adjust or view any such system if it will distract your attention while you are driving; you **MUST** exercise proper control of your vehicle at all times. If necessary, find a safe place to stop first.
*Laws RTO 1995 Arts 10 & 12 & CUR reg 120*

### In slow moving traffic

**129.** You should

- reduce the distance between you and the vehicle ahead to maintain traffic flow
- never get so close to the vehicle in front that you cannot stop safely
- leave enough space to be able to manoeuvre if the vehicle in front breaks down or an emergency vehicle needs to get past
- not change lanes to the left to overtake
- allow access into and from side roads, as blocking these will add to congestion.

Do not block access to a side road

### Driving in built-up areas

**130. Narrow residential streets.** You should drive slowly and carefully on streets where there are likely to be pedestrians, cyclists and parked cars. In some areas a 20 mph maximum speed limit may be in force. Look out for

- vehicles emerging from junctions
- vehicles moving off

- car doors opening
- pedestrians
- children running out from between parked vehicles
- cyclists and motorcyclists.

**131. Traffic calming measures.** On some roads there are features such as road humps, chicanes and narrowings which are intended to slow you down. When you approach these features reduce your speed. Allow cyclists and motorcyclists room to pass through them. Maintain a reduced speed along the whole of the stretch of road within the calming measures. Give way to oncoming traffic if directed to do so by signs. You should not overtake other moving vehicles whilst in these areas.

Chicanes may be used to slow traffic down

## Country roads
**132.** Take extra care on country roads and reduce your speed at approaches to bends, which can be sharper than they appear, and at minor junctions and turnings, which may be partially hidden. Be prepared for pedestrians, horse riders and cyclists walking or riding in the road. You should also reduce your speed where country roads enter villages.

**133. Single-track roads.** These are only wide enough for one vehicle. They may have special passing places. If you see a vehicle coming towards you, or the driver behind wants to overtake, pull into a passing place on your left, or wait opposite a passing place on your right. Give way to vehicles coming uphill whenever you can. If necessary, reverse until you reach a passing place to let the other vehicle pass.

**134.** Do not park in passing places.

# Using the road

## General rules

**135. Before moving off** you should

- use all mirrors to check the road is clear
- look round to check the blind spots (the areas you are unable to see in the mirrors)
- signal if necessary before moving out
- look round for a final check.

Move off only when it is safe to do so.

Check the blind spot before moving off

**136. Once moving** you should

- keep to the left, unless road signs or markings indicate otherwise. The exceptions are when you want to overtake, turn right or pass parked vehicles or pedestrians in the road
- keep well to the left on right-hand bends. This will improve your view of the road and help avoid the risk of colliding with traffic approaching from the opposite direction
- keep both hands on the wheel, where possible. This will help you to remain in full control of the vehicle at all times
- be aware of other vehicles especially cycles and motorcycles. These are more difficult to see than larger vehicles and their riders are particularly vulnerable. Give them plenty of room, especially if you are driving a long vehicle or towing a trailer
- select a lower gear before you reach a long downhill slope. This will help to control your speed
- when towing, remember the extra length will affect overtaking and manoeuvring. The extra weight will also affect the braking and acceleration.

### Mirrors

**137.** All mirrors should be used effectively throughout your journey. You should

- use your mirrors frequently so that you always know what is behind and to each side of you
- use them in good time before you signal or change direction or speed
- be aware that mirrors do not cover all areas and there will be blind spots. You will need to look round and check.

**Remember: Mirrors – Signal – Manoeuvre**

## Overtaking

**138. Before overtaking** you should make sure

- the road is sufficiently clear ahead
- the vehicle behind is not beginning to overtake you
- there is a suitable gap in front of the vehicle you plan to overtake.

**139. Overtake only** when it is safe to do so. You should

- not get too close to the vehicle you intend to overtake
- use your mirrors, signal when it is safe to do so, take a quick sideways glance into the blind spot area and then start to move out
- not assume that you can simply follow a vehicle ahead which is overtaking; there may only be enough room for one vehicle
- move quickly past the vehicle you are overtaking, once you have started to overtake. Allow plenty of room. Move back to the left as soon as you can but do not cut in
- take extra care at night and in poor visibility when it is harder to judge speed and distance
- give way to oncoming vehicles before passing parked vehicles or other obstructions on your side of the road
- only overtake on the left if the vehicle in front is signalling to turn right, and there is room to do so
- stay in your lane if traffic is moving slowly in queues. If the queue on your right is moving more slowly than you are, you may pass on the left
- give motorcyclists, cyclists and horse riders at least as much room as you would a car when overtaking (see Rules 188, 189 and 191).

**Remember: Mirrors – Signal – Manoeuvre**

Do not cut in too quickly

**140. Large vehicles.** Overtaking these is more difficult. You should

- drop back to increase your ability to see ahead. Getting too close to large vehicles will obscure your view of the road ahead and there may be another slow moving vehicle in front
- make sure that you have enough room to complete your overtaking manoeuvre before committing yourself. It takes longer to pass a large vehicle. If in doubt do not overtake
- not assume you can follow a vehicle ahead which is overtaking a long vehicle. If a problem develops, they may abort overtaking and pull back in.

**141.** You **MUST NOT** overtake

- if you would have to cross or straddle double white lines with a solid line nearest to you (but see Rule 108)
- if you would have to enter an area designed to divide traffic, if it is surrounded by a solid white line
- the nearest vehicle to a pedestrian crossing, especially when it has stopped to let pedestrians cross
- if you would have to enter a lane reserved for buses, trams or cycles during its hours of operation
- after a 'No Overtaking' sign and until you pass a sign cancelling the restriction.

*Laws RTO 1995 Art 49, TSR reg 8, ZPCR reg 10*

**142. DO NOT** overtake if there is any doubt, or where you cannot see far enough ahead to be sure it is safe. For example, when you are approaching
- a corner or bend
- a hump bridge
- the brow of a hill.

**143. DO NOT** overtake where you might come into conflict with other road users. For example
- approaching or at a road junction on either side of the road
- where the road narrows
- when approaching a school crossing patrol
- between the kerb and a bus or tram when it is at a stop
- where traffic is queuing at junctions or road works
- when you would force another vehicle to swerve or slow down
- at a level crossing
- when a vehicle is indicating right, even if you believe the signal should have been cancelled. Do not take a risk; wait for the signal to be cancelled.

**144. Being overtaken.** If a driver is trying to overtake you, maintain a steady course and speed, slowing down if necessary to let the vehicle pass. Never obstruct drivers who wish to pass. Speeding up or driving unpredictably while someone is overtaking you is dangerous. Drop back to maintain a two-second gap if someone overtakes and pulls into the gap in front of you.

**145.** Do not hold up a long queue of traffic, especially if you are driving a large or slow moving vehicle. Check your mirrors frequently, and if necessary, pull in where it is safe and let traffic pass.

## Road junctions

**146.** Take extra care at junctions. You should
- watch out for cyclists, motorcyclists and pedestrians as they are not always easy to see
- watch out for pedestrians crossing a road into which you are turning. If they have started to cross they have priority, so give way

- watch out for long vehicles which may be turning at a junction ahead; they may have to use the whole width of the road to make the turn (see Rule 196)
- not assume, when waiting at a junction, that a vehicle coming from the right and signalling left will actually turn. Wait and make sure
- not cross or join a road until there is a gap large enough for you to do so safely.

**147.** You **MUST** stop behind the line at a junction with a 'Stop' sign and a solid white line across the road. Wait for a safe gap in the traffic before you move off.
*Laws RTO 1995 Art 49 & TSR regs 8 & 14*

**148.** The approach to a junction may have a 'Give Way' sign or a triangle marked on the road. You **MUST** give way to traffic on the main road when emerging from a junction with broken white lines across the road.
*Law RTO 1995 Art 49 & TSR regs 8 & 24*

**149. Dual carriageways.** When crossing or turning right, first assess whether the central reservation is deep enough to protect the full length of your vehicle.
- If it is, then you should treat each half of the carriageway as a separate road. Wait in the central reservation until there is a safe gap in the traffic on the second half of the road.
- If the central reservation is too shallow for the length of your vehicle, wait until you can cross both carriageways in one go.

Assess your vehicle's length and do not obstruct traffic

**150. Box junctions.** These have criss-cross yellow lines painted on the road (see page 80). You **MUST NOT** enter the box until your exit road or lane is clear. However, you may enter the box and wait when you want to turn right, and are only stopped from doing so by oncoming traffic, or by other vehicles waiting to turn right.
*Law TSR regs 8(1) & 26*

Enter a box junction only if your exit road is clear

## Junctions controlled by traffic lights

**151.** You **MUST** stop behind the white 'Stop' line across your side of the road unless the light is green. If the amber light appears you may go on only if you have already crossed the stop line or are so close to it that to stop might cause an accident.
*Law TSR regs 8 & 33*

**152.** You **MUST NOT** move forward over the white line when the red light is showing. Only go forward when the traffic lights are green if there is room for you to clear the junction safely or you are taking up a position to turn right. If the traffic lights are not working, proceed with caution.
*Law TSR regs 8 & 33*

**153. Green filter arrow.** This indicates a filter lane only. Do not enter that lane unless you want to go in the direction of the arrow. If it is safe to do so, you may proceed in the direction of the green arrow when it, or the full green light shows. Give other traffic, especially cyclists, time and room to move into the correct lane.

**154. Advanced stop lines.** Some junctions have advanced stop lines or bus advance areas to allow cycles and buses to be positioned ahead of other traffic. Motorists **MUST** wait behind the first white line reached, and not encroach on the marked area. Allow cyclists and buses time and space to move off when the green signal shows.

*Laws RTO 1995 Art 50, TSR reg 33(6)*

Do not encroach on the area marked for cyclists

## Turning right

**155. Well before** you turn right you should

- use your mirrors to make sure you know the position and movement of traffic behind you
- give a right-turn signal
- take up a position just left of the middle of the road or in the space marked for traffic turning right
- leave room for other vehicles to pass on the left, if possible.

Position your vehicle correctly to avoid obstructing traffic

**156.** Wait until there is a safe gap between you and any oncoming vehicle. Watch out for cyclists, motorcyclists and pedestrians. Check your mirrors and blind spot again to make sure you are not being overtaken, then make the turn. Do not cut the corner. Take great care when turning into a main road; you will need to watch for traffic in both directions and wait for a safe gap.

**Remember: Mirrors – Signal – Manoeuvre**

**157. When turning** at a cross roads where an oncoming vehicle is also turning right, there is a choice of two methods

- turn right side to right side; keep the other vehicle on your right and turn behind it. This is generally the safest method as you have a clear view of any approaching traffic when completing your turn
- left side to left side, turning in front of each other. This can block your view of oncoming vehicles, so take extra care.

Road layout, markings or how the other vehicle is positioned can determine which course should be taken.

Turning right side to right side

Turning left side to left side

## Turning left

**158.** Use your mirrors and give a left-turn signal well before you turn left. Do not overtake just before you turn left and watch out for traffic coming up on your left before you make the turn, especially if driving a large vehicle. Cyclists and motorcyclists in particular may be hidden from your view.

Do not cut in on cyclists

**159.** When turning
- keep as close to the left as is safe and practical
- give way to any vehicles using a bus lane, cycle lane or tramway from either direction.

## Roundabouts

**160. On approaching a roundabout** take notice and act on all the information available to you, including traffic signs, traffic lights and lane markings which direct you into the correct lane. You should
- use **Mirrors – Signal – Manoeuvre** at all stages
- decide as early as possible which exit you need to take
- give an appropriate signal (see Rule 162). Time your signals so as not to confuse other road users
- get into the correct lane
- adjust your speed and position to fit in with traffic conditions
- be aware of the speed and position of all the traffic around you.

Follow the correct procedure at roundabouts

**161. When reaching the roundabout** you should
- give priority to traffic approaching from your right, unless directed otherwise by signs, road markings or traffic lights
- check whether road markings allow you to enter the roundabout without giving way. If so, proceed, but still look to the right before joining
- watch out for vehicles already on the roundabout; be aware they may not be signalling correctly or at all
- look forward before moving off to make sure traffic in front has moved off.

**162. Signals and position,** unless signs or markings indicate otherwise.

When taking the first exit
- signal left and approach in the left-hand lane
- keep to the left on the roundabout and continue signalling left to leave.

When taking any intermediate exit
- select the appropriate lane on approach to and on the roundabout, signalling as necessary
- stay in this lane until you need to alter course to exit the roundabout
- signal left after you have passed the exit before the one you want.

When taking the last exit or going full circle
- signal right and approach in the right-hand lane
- keep to the right on the roundabout until you need to change lanes to exit the roundabout
- signal left after you have passed the exit before the one you want.

When there are more than three lanes at the entrance to a roundabout, use the most appropriate lane on approach and through it.

For more specific advice on procedures at roundabouts, see Appendix on pages 94-97

**163. In all cases watch out for** and give plenty of room to
- pedestrians who may be crossing the approach and exit roads
- traffic crossing in front of you on the roundabout, especially vehicles intending to leave by the next exit
- traffic which may be straddling lanes or positioned incorrectly
- motorcyclists
- cyclists and horse riders who may stay in the left-hand lane and signal right if they intend to continue round the roundabout
- long vehicles (including those towing trailers) which might have to take a different course approaching or on the roundabout because of their length. Watch out for their signals.

**164. Mini-roundabouts.** Approach these in the same way as normal roundabouts. All vehicles **MUST** pass round the central markings except large vehicles which are physically incapable of doing so. Remember, there is less space to manoeuvre and less time to signal. Beware of vehicles making U-turns.
*Law RTO 1995 Art 50, TSR reg 8*

**165.** At double mini-roundabouts treat each roundabout separately and give way to traffic from the right.

Treat each roundabout separately

**166. Multiple roundabouts.** At some complex junctions there may be a series of mini-roundabouts at the intersections. Treat each mini-roundabout separately and follow the normal rules.

## Pedestrian crossings

**167.** You **MUST NOT** park on a crossing or in the area covered by the zigzag lines. You **MUST NOT** overtake the moving vehicle nearest the crossing or the vehicle nearest the crossing which has stopped to give way to pedestrians.
*Laws ZPCR regs 10 & 12 & RTRO Art 59(4)*

**168.** In queuing traffic, you should keep the crossing clear.

Keep the crossing clear

**169.** You should take extra care where the view of either side of the crossing is blocked by queuing traffic or incorrectly parked vehicles. Pedestrians may be crossing between stationary vehicles.

**170.** Allow pedestrians plenty of time to cross and do not harass them by revving your engine or edging forward.

**171. Zebra crossings.** As you approach a zebra crossing
- look out for people waiting to cross and be ready to slow down or stop to let them cross
- you **MUST** give way when someone has moved onto a crossing
- allow more time for stopping on wet or icy roads
- do not wave people across; this could be dangerous if another vehicle is approaching
- be aware of pedestrians approaching from the side of the crossing.

*Laws ZPCR reg 8 & RTRO Art 59(4)*

## Signal-controlled crossings
**172. Pelican crossings.** These are signal-controlled crossings where a flashing amber light follows the red 'Stop' light. You **MUST** stop when the red light shows. When the amber light is flashing, you **MUST** give way to any pedestrians on the crossing. If the amber light is flashing and there are no pedestrians on the crossing, you may proceed with caution.

*Laws PPCR reg 13 & RTRO Art 59(4)*

Allow pedestrians to cross when the amber light is flashing

**173.** Pelican crossings which go straight across the road are one crossing, even when there is a central island. You **MUST** wait for pedestrians who are crossing from the other side of the island.

*Laws PPCR reg 13 & RTRO Art 59(4)*

**174.** Give way to pedestrians who are still crossing after the signal for vehicles has changed to green.

**175. Toucan and puffin crossings.** These are similar to pelican crossings, but there is no flashing amber phase.

## Reversing

**176.** Choose an appropriate place to manoeuvre. If you need to turn your car around, wait until you find a safe place. Try not to reverse or turn round in a busy road; find a quiet side road or drive round a block of side streets.

**177.** Do not reverse from a side road into a main road. When using a driveway, reverse in and drive out if you can.

**178.** Look carefully before you start reversing. You should
- use all your mirrors
- check the 'blind spot' behind you (the part of the road you cannot see easily in the mirrors)
- check there are no pedestrians, particularly children, cyclists, or obstructions in the road behind you
- look mainly through the rear window
- check all around just before you start to turn and be aware that the front of your vehicle will swing out as you turn
- get someone to guide you if you cannot see clearly.

Check all round when reversing

**179.** You **MUST NOT** reverse your vehicle further than necessary.
*Law CUR reg 122*

# Road users requiring extra care

**180.** The most vulnerable road users are pedestrians, cyclists, motorcyclists and horse riders. It is particularly important to be aware of children, elderly and disabled people, and learner and inexperienced drivers and riders.

## Pedestrians
**181.** In urban areas there is a risk of pedestrians, especially children, stepping unexpectedly into the road. You should drive with the safety of children in mind at a speed suitable for the conditions.

**182. Drive carefully and slowly** when
- in crowded shopping streets or residential areas
- driving past bus and tram stops; pedestrians may emerge suddenly into the road
- passing parked vehicles, especially ice cream vans; children are more interested in ice cream than traffic and may run into the road unexpectedly
- needing to cross a footpath or footway; for example, to reach a driveway. Give way to pedestrians on the footpath or footway
- reversing into a side road; look all around the vehicle and give way to any pedestrians who may be crossing the road
- turning at road junctions; give way to pedestrians who are already crossing the road into which you are turning
- the footpath or footway is closed due to street repairs and pedestrians are directed to use the road.

Watch out for children in busy areas

**183. Particularly vulnerable pedestrians.** These include
- children and elderly pedestrians who may not be able to judge your speed and could step into the road in front of you. At 40 mph your vehicle will probably kill any pedestrians it hits. At 20 mph there is only a 1 in 20 chance

of the pedestrian being killed. So kill your speed

- elderly pedestrians who may need more time to cross the road. Be patient and allow them to cross in their own time. Do not hurry them by revving your engine or edging forward
- blind and partially sighted people who may be carrying a white cane (white with a red band for deaf and blind people) or using a guide dog
- people with disabilities. Those with hearing problems may not be aware of your vehicle approaching. Those with walking difficulties require more time.

**184. Near schools.** Drive slowly and be particularly aware of young cyclists and pedestrians. In some places, there may be a flashing amber signal below the 'Patrol' or 'School' warning sign which tells you that there may be children crossing the road ahead. Drive very slowly until you are clear of the area.

**185.** Drive carefully when passing a stationary bus carrying school children or showing 'School Bus' markings or signs (see page 81) as children may be getting on or off.

**186.** You **MUST** stop when a school crossing patrol shows a 'Stop' for children sign (see page 73).
*Law RTRO Art 60*

## Motorcyclists and cyclists

**187.** It is often difficult to see motorcyclists and cyclists especially when they are coming up from behind, coming out of junctions and at roundabouts. Always look out for them when you are emerging from a junction.

Look out for motorcyclists at junctions

**188.** When passing motorcyclists and cyclists, give them plenty of room (see Rule 139). If they look over their shoulder whilst you are following them it could mean that they may soon attempt to turn right. Give them time and space to do so.

**189.** Motorcyclists and cyclists may suddenly need to avoid uneven road surfaces and obstacles such as draincovers or oily, wet or icy patches on the road. Give them plenty of room.

## Other road users
**190. Animals.** When passing animals, drive slowly. Give them plenty of room and be ready to stop. Do not scare animals by sounding your horn or revving your engine. Look out for animals being led or ridden on the road and take extra care and keep your speed down at left-hand bends and on narrow country roads. If a road is blocked by a herd of animals, stop and switch off your engine until they have left the road. Watch out for animals on unfenced roads.

**191. Horse riders.** Be particularly careful of horses and riders, especially when overtaking. Always pass wide and slow. Horse riders are often children, so take extra care and remember riders may ride in double file when escorting a young or inexperienced horse rider. Look out for horse riders' signals and heed a request to slow down or stop. Treat all horses as a potential hazard and take great care.

**192. Elderly drivers.** Their reactions may be slower than other drivers. Make allowance for this.

**193. Learners and inexperienced drivers.** They may not be so skilful at reacting to events. Be particularly patient with learner, restricted and young drivers. Drivers who have recently passed their test are required to display R plates for one year, not counting any periods of disqualification or revocation.

## Other vehicles
**194. Emergency vehicles.** You should look and listen for ambulances, fire engines, police or other emergency vehicles using flashing blue, red or green lights, headlights or sirens. When one approaches do not panic. Consider the route of the emergency vehicle and take appropriate action to let it pass. If necessary, pull to the side of the road and stop, but do not endanger other road users.

**195. Powered vehicles used by disabled people.** These small vehicles travel at a maximum speed of 8 mph. On a dual carriageway they **MUST** have a flashing amber light, but on other roads you may not have that advance warning.
*Law RVLR reg 20(1)*

**196. Large vehicles.** These may need extra road space to turn or to deal with a hazard that you are not able to see. If you are following a large vehicle, such as a bus or articulated lorry, be prepared to stop and wait if it needs room or time to turn.

Long vehicles need extra room

**197.** Large vehicles can block your view. Your ability to see and to plan ahead will be improved if you pull back to increase your separation distance.

**198. Buses, coaches and trams.** Give priority to these vehicles when you can do so safely, especially when they signal to pull away from stops. Look out for people getting off a bus or tram and crossing the road.

**199. Electric vehicles.** Be careful of electric vehicles such as milk floats and trams. Trams move quickly but silently and cannot steer to avoid you.

**200. Vehicles with flashing amber lights.** These warn of a slow-moving vehicle (such as a road gritter or recovery vehicle) or a vehicle which has broken down, so approach with caution.

# Driving in adverse weather conditions

**201.** You **MUST** use headlights when visibility is seriously reduced, generally when you cannot see for more than 100 metres (328 feet). You may also use front or rear fog lights (in addition to headlights) but you **MUST** switch them off when visibility improves (see Rule 211).

*Law RVLR regs 28 & 30*

## Wet weather

**202.** In wet weather, stopping distances will be at least double those required for stopping on dry roads (see pages 27–29). This is because your tyres have less grip on the road. In wet weather

- you should keep well back from the vehicle in front. This will increase your ability to see and plan ahead
- if the steering becomes unresponsive, it probably means that water is preventing the tyres from gripping the road. Ease off the accelerator and slow down gradually
- the rain and spray from vehicles may make it difficult to see and be seen.

## Icy and snowy weather

**203.** In winter check the local weather forecast for warnings of icy or snowy weather. **DO NOT** drive in these conditions unless your journey is essential. If it is, take great care. Carry a spade, warm clothing, a warm drink and emergency food in case your vehicle breaks down or cannot proceed.

**204.** Before you set off
- you **MUST** be able to see, so clear all snow and ice from all your windows
- you **MUST** ensure that lights and number plates are clean
- make sure the mirrors are clear and the windows are de-misted thoroughly.

*Laws CUR reg 35 & RVLR reg 26*

Make sure your windscreen is completely clear

**205.  When driving** in icy or snowy weather
- drive with care, even if the roads have been gritted
- keep well back from the vehicle in front as stopping distances can be ten times greater than on dry roads
- take care when overtaking gritting vehicles, particularly if you are riding a motorcycle
- watch out for snowploughs which may throw out snow on either side. Do not overtake them unless the lane you intend to use has been cleared
- be prepared for the road conditions changing over relatively short distances.

**206.  Drive extremely carefully** when the roads are icy. Avoid sudden actions as these could cause a skid. You should
- drive at a slow speed in as high a gear as possible; accelerate and brake very gently
- drive particularly slowly on bends where skids are more likely. Brake progressively on the straight before you reach a bend. Having slowed down, steer smoothly round the bend, avoiding sudden actions
- check your grip on the road surface when there is snow or ice by choosing a safe place to brake gently. If the steering feels unresponsive this may indicate ice and your vehicle losing its grip on the road. When travelling on ice, tyres make virtually no noise.

## Windy weather
**207.**  High sided vehicles are most affected by windy weather, but strong gusts can also blow a car, cyclist or motorcyclist off course. This can happen at open stretches of road exposed to strong cross winds, or when passing bridges or gaps in hedges.

**208.**  In very windy weather your vehicle may be affected by turbulence created by large vehicles. Motorcyclists are particularly affected, so keep well back from them when they are overtaking a high-sided vehicle.

## Fog
**209.  Before entering fog** check your mirrors then slow down. If the word 'Fog' is shown on a roadside signal or overhead gantry but the road is clear, be prepared for a bank of fog or drifting patchy fog ahead. Even if it seems to be clearing, you can suddenly find yourself in thick fog.

**210.  When driving in fog** you should
- use your lights as required in Rule 201
- keep a safe distance behind the vehicle in front. Rear lights can give a false sense of security
- be able to pull up within the distance you can see clearly. This is particularly important on motorways and dual carriageways, as vehicles are travelling faster
- use your windscreen wipers and demisters
- beware of other drivers not using headlights
- not accelerate to get away from a vehicle which is too close behind you
- check your mirrors before you slow down.  Then use your brakes so that your brake lights warn drivers behind you that you are slowing down
- stop in the correct position at a junction with limited visibility and listen for traffic. When you are sure it is safe to emerge, do so positively and do not hesitate in a position that puts you directly in the path of approaching vehicles.

**211.**  You **MUST NOT** use front or rear fog lights unless visibility is seriously reduced (see Rule 201) as they dazzle other road users and can obscure your brake lights. You **MUST** switch them off when visibility improves.
*Law RVLR regs 28 & 30*

## Hot weather
**212.**  Keep your vehicle well ventilated to avoid drowsiness.  Be aware that the road surface may become soft or if it rains after a dry spell it may become slippery. These conditions could affect your steering and braking.

# Waiting and parking

**213.**  You **MUST NOT** wait or park where there are restrictions shown by
- yellow lines along the edge of the carriageway (see page 79). The periods when restrictions apply are shown on upright signs usually at intervals along the road, parallel to the kerb
- bus stop markings on the carriageway unless otherwise indicated by signs
- school entrance markings on the carriageway when the markings are accompanied by signs indicating a prohibition on stopping during certain periods.  In all other

circumstances, you should not wait or park where there are school entrance markings on the carriageway.

*Laws RTRO Art 4(5) & R(RW)O*

## Parking

**214.** Use off-street parking areas, or bays marked out with white lines on the road as parking places, wherever possible. If you have to stop on the road side

- stop as close as you can to the side
- do not stop too close to a vehicle displaying a Blue Badge; remember, the vehicle occupants may need more room to get in or out
- you **MUST** switch off the engine, headlights and fog lights
- you **MUST** apply the handbrake before leaving the vehicle
- you **MUST** ensure you do not hit anyone when you open your door
- it is safer for your passengers (especially children) to get out of the vehicle on the side next to the kerb
- lock your vehicle.

*Laws CUR regs 113, 121 & 123  RVLR reg 30 & RTO 1995 Art 58*

Check before opening your door

**215.** You **MUST NOT** stop or park on

- the carriageway or the hard shoulder of a motorway except in an emergency (see Rule 244)
- a pedestrian crossing, including the area marked by the zigzag lines (see Rule 167)
- within 15 metres (50ft) of any junction, except in a lay-by in specified circumstances or in a designated parking area
- a Clearway (see page 73)
- an Urban Clearway within its hours of operation, except to pick up or set down passengers (see page 73)
- a road marked with double white lines, except to pick up or set down passengers

- a bus stop marked on the carriageway unless otherwise indicated by signs
- a bus, tram or cycle lane during its period of operation
- a cycle track.

*Laws RTO 1995 Art 32, CUR reg 119 & R(RW)O*

**216.** You **MUST NOT** park in parking spaces reserved for specific users, such as Blue Badge holders or residents, unless entitled to do so.

*Laws RTRO Art14(1) &19(1)*

**217. DO NOT** park your vehicle or trailer on the road where it would endanger, inconvenience or obstruct pedestrians or other road users. For example, do not stop
- near a school entrance
- anywhere you would prevent access for Emergency Services
- at or near a bus stop or taxi rank
- on the approach to a level crossing
- near the brow of a hill or hump bridge
- opposite a traffic island or (if this would cause an obstruction) another parked vehicle
- where you would force other traffic to enter a tram lane
- where the kerb has been lowered to help wheelchair users
- in front of an entrance to a property
- on a bend.

**218. DO NOT** park partially or wholly on the footpath or footway unless signs permit it. Parking on the footpath or footway can obstruct and seriously inconvenience pedestrians, people in wheelchairs, the visually impaired and people with prams or pushchairs.

**219. Controlled parking zones.** The zone entry signs indicate the times when the waiting restrictions within the zone are in force. Parking may be allowed in some places at other times. Otherwise parking will be within separately signed and marked bays.

**220. Goods vehicles.** Vehicles with a maximum laden weight of over 7.5 tonnes (including any trailer) **MUST NOT** be parked on a verge, footpath or footway or any land situated between carriageways, without police permission. The only exception is when parking is essential for loading and unloading, in which case the vehicle **MUST NOT** be left unattended.

*Law RTO 1995 Art 30(1)*

**221. Loading and unloading.** Do not load or unload where there are yellow markings on the kerb and upright signs advise restrictions are in place (see page 80). This may be permitted where parking is otherwise restricted.
*Law RTRO Art 4(5)*

## Parking at night
**222.** You **MUST NOT** park on a road at night (between half an hour after sunset and half an hour before sunrise) facing against the direction of the traffic flow unless in a recognised parking space.
*Law CUR reg 117*

**223.** Between sunset and sunrise all vehicles **MUST** display parking lights when parked on a road or a lay-by on a road with a speed limit greater than 30 mph.
*Law RVLR reg 27*

**224.** Cars, goods vehicles not exceeding 1525kg unladen, invalid carriages and motorcycles may be parked without lights on a road (or lay-by) with a speed limit of 30 mph or less if they are
- at least 15 metres (50 feet) away from any junction, close to the kerb and facing in the direction of the traffic flow
- in a recognised parking place or lay-by.

Other vehicles and trailers, and all vehicles with projecting loads, **MUST NOT** be left on a road at night without lights.
*Law RVLR reg 27 & R(RW)O*

**225. Parking in fog.** It is especially dangerous to park on the road in fog. If it is unavoidable, leave your parking lights or sidelights on.

**226. Parking on hills.** If you park on a hill you should
- park close to the kerb and apply the handbrake firmly
- select a forward gear and turn your steering wheel away from the kerb when facing uphill
- select reverse gear and turn your steering wheel towards the kerb when facing downhill
- use 'park' if your car has an automatic gearbox.

# Motorways

Many other Rules also apply to motorway driving, either wholly or in part: Rules 43, 67–105, 109–113, 118, 122, 126–128, 135, 137, 194, 196, 200, 201–212, 248–252, 254–264.

## General

**227. Prohibited vehicles.** Motorways MUST NOT be used by pedestrians, holders of provisional car or motorcycle driving licences unless exempt, riders of motorcycles under 50cc, cyclists and horse riders. Certain slow-moving vehicles and those carrying oversized loads (except by special permission), agricultural vehicles and most invalid carriages are also prohibited.
*Laws RO Art 16 & Sch 1 & MTR reg 3*

**228.** Traffic on motorways usually travels faster than on other roads, so you have less time to react. It is especially important to use your mirrors earlier and look much further ahead than you would on other roads.

### Motorway signals
**229.** Motorway signals (see page 70) are used to warn you of a danger ahead. For example, there may be an accident, fog or a spillage, which you may not immediately be able to see.

**230.** Signals situated on the central reservation apply to all lanes. On very busy stretches, signals may be overhead with a separate signal for each lane.

**231. Amber flashing lights.** These warn of a hazard ahead. The signal may show a temporary maximum speed limit, lanes that are closed or a message such as 'Fog'. Adjust your speed and look out for the danger until you pass a signal which is not flashing or one that gives the 'All clear' sign and you are sure it is safe to increase your speed.

**232. Red flashing lights.** If red lights on the overhead signals flash above your lane (there may also be a red 'X') you MUST NOT go beyond the signal in that lane. If red lights flash on a signal in the central reservation or at the side of the road, you MUST NOT go beyond the signal in any lane.
*Laws RTO 1995 Art 49 & TSR reg 8*

# Driving on the motorway

## Joining the motorway

**233.** When you join the motorway you will normally approach it from a road on the left (a slip road) or from an adjoining motorway. You should

- give priority to traffic already on the motorway
- check the traffic on the motorway and adjust your speed to fit safely into the traffic flow in the left-hand lane
- not cross solid white lines that separate lanes
- stay on the slip road if it continues as an extra lane on the motorway
- remain in the left-hand lane long enough to adjust to the speed of traffic before considering overtaking.

## On the motorway

**234.** When you can see well ahead and the road conditions are good, you should

- drive at a steady cruising speed which you and your vehicle can handle safely and is within the speed limit (see table on page 26)
- keep a safe distance from the vehicle in front and increase the gap on wet or icy roads, or in fog (see Rules 105 & 210).

**235.** You **MUST NOT** exceed 70 mph, or the maximum speed limit permitted for your vehicle (see page 26). If a lower speed limit is in force, either permanently or temporarily, at roadworks for example, you **MUST NOT** exceed the lower limit. On some motorways, mandatory motorway signals (which display the speed limit within a red ring) are used to vary the maximum speed limit to improve traffic flow. You **MUST NOT** exceed this speed limit.
*Laws RO Art 20, RTRO Art 39 & MV(SL)R*

**236.** The monotony of driving on a motorway can make you feel sleepy. To minimise the risk, follow the advice in Rule 80.

**237.** You **MUST NOT** reverse, cross the central reservation, or drive against the traffic flow. If you have missed your exit, or have taken the wrong route, carry on to the next exit.
*Law MTR regs 5, 8 & 10*

## Lane discipline

**238.** You should drive in the left-hand lane if the road ahead is clear. If you are overtaking a number of slower moving vehicles it may be safer to remain in the centre or outer lanes until the manoeuvre is completed rather than continuously switching lanes. Return to the left lane once you have overtaken all the vehicles or if you are delaying traffic behind you. Slow moving or speed restricted vehicles should always remain in the left lane of the carriageway unless overtaking. You **MUST NOT** drive on the hard shoulder except in an emergency or if directed to by signs.

*Law MTR reg 4 & 9*

**239.** The right-hand lane of a motorway with three or more lanes should not be used if you are driving

- any vehicle drawing a trailer
- a goods vehicle with a maximum laden weight over 7.5 tonnes
- a passenger vehicle with a maximum laden weight exceeding 7.5 tonnes constructed or adapted to carry more than eight seated passengers in addition to the driver.

**240. Approaching a junction.** Look well ahead for signals or signs. Direction signs may be placed over the road. If you need to change lanes, do so in good time. At some junctions a lane may lead directly off the motorway. Only get in that lane if you wish to go in the direction indicated on the overhead signs.

## Overtaking

**241.** Do not overtake unless you are sure it is safe to do so. Overtake only on the right. You should

- check your mirrors
- take time to judge the speeds correctly
- make sure that the lane you will be joining is sufficiently clear ahead and behind
- take a quick sideways glance into the blind spot area to verify the position of a vehicle that may have disappeared from your view in the mirror
- remember that traffic may be coming up behind you very quickly. Check your mirrors carefully. When it is safe to do so, signal in plenty of time, then move out
- ensure you do not cut in on the vehicle you have overtaken
- be especially careful at night and in poor visibility when it is harder to judge speed and distance.

**242.** Do not overtake on the left or move to a lane on your left to overtake. In congested conditions, where adjacent lanes of traffic are moving at similar speeds, traffic in left-hand lanes may sometimes be moving faster than traffic to the right. In these conditions you may keep up with the traffic in your lane even if this means passing traffic in the lane to your right. Do not weave in and out of lanes to overtake.

**243.** You **MUST NOT** use the hard shoulder for overtaking.
*Law MTR regs 4 & 9*

## Stopping
**244.** You **MUST NOT** stop on the carriageway, hard shoulder, slip road, central reservation or verge except in an emergency, or when told to do so by the police, an emergency sign or by flashing red light signals.
*Law MTR regs 6, 9 & 10*

**245.** You **MUST NOT** pick up or set down anyone, or walk on a motorway, except in an emergency.
*Laws RO Art 20 & MTR reg 13*

## Leaving the motorway
**246.** Unless signs indicate that a lane leads directly off the motorway, you will normally leave the motorway by a slip road on your left. You should
- watch for the signs letting you know you are getting near your exit
- move into the left-hand lane well before reaching your exit
- signal left in good time and reduce your speed on the slip road as necessary.

**247.** On leaving the motorway or using a link road between motorways, your speed may be higher than you realise - 50 mph may feel like 30 mph. Check your speedometer and adjust your speed accordingly. Some slip roads and link roads have sharp bends, so you will need to slow down.

# Breakdowns and collisions

## Breakdowns

**248.** If your vehicle breaks down, think first of other road users and

- get your vehicle off the road if possible
- warn other traffic by using your hazard warning lights if your vehicle is causing an obstruction
- put a warning triangle on the road at least 45 metres (147 feet) behind your broken-down vehicle on the same side of the road, or use other permitted warning devices if you have them. Always take great care when placing them
- keep your sidelights on if it is dark or visibility is poor
- do not stand (or let anybody else stand), between your vehicle and oncoming traffic
- at night or in poor visibility do not stand where you will prevent other road users seeing your lights.

### Additional rules for the motorway

**249.** If your vehicle develops a problem, leave the motorway at the next exit or pull into a service area. If you cannot do so, you should

- pull on to the hard shoulder and stop as far to the left as possible, with your wheels turned to the left
- try to stop near an emergency telephone (situated at approximately one mile intervals along the hard shoulder)
- leave the vehicle by the left-hand door and ensure your passengers do the same. You MUST leave any animals in the vehicle or, in an emergency, keep them under proper control on the verge
- not attempt even simple repairs
- ensure that passengers keep away from the carriageway and hard shoulder, and that children are kept under control
- walk to an emergency telephone on your side of the carriageway (follow the arrows on the posts at the back of the hard shoulder) – the telephone is free of charge and connects directly to the police. Use these in preference to a mobile phone (see Rule 257)
- give full details to the police; also inform them if you are a vulnerable motorist such as a woman travelling alone
- return and wait near your vehicle (well away from the carriageway and hard shoulder)
- if you feel at risk from another person, return to your vehicle

by a left-hand door and lock all doors. Leave your vehicle
again as soon as you feel this danger has passed.

*Laws MTR regs 12 & 13*

Keep well back from the hard shoulder

**250.** Before you rejoin the carriageway after a breakdown,
build up speed on the hard shoulder and watch for a safe gap
in the traffic. Be aware that other vehicles may be stationary on
the hard shoulder.

**251.** If you cannot get your vehicle on to the hard shoulder
- do not attempt to place any warning triangle on the
  carriageway
- switch on your hazard warning lights
- leave your vehicle only when you can safely get clear of the
  carriageway.

## Disabled drivers

**252.** If you have a disability which prevents you from following
the above advice you should
- stay in your vehicle
- switch on your hazard warning lights
- display a 'Help' pennant or, if you have a car or mobile
  phone, contact the emergency services and be prepared
  to advise them of your location.

## Obstructions

**253.** If anything falls from your vehicle (or any other vehicle) on
to the road, stop and retrieve it only if it is safe to do so.

**254. Motorways.** On a motorway do not try to remove the
obstruction yourself. Stop at the next emergency telephone
and call the police.

# Collisions

**255. Warning signs or flashing lights.** If you see or hear emergency vehicles in the distance be aware there may be a collision ahead.

**256.** When passing the scene of a collision do not be distracted or slow down unnecessarily (for example if a collision is on the other side of a dual carriageway). This may cause another collision or traffic congestion, but see Rule 257.

**257.** If you are involved in a collision or stop to give assistance
- use your hazard warning lights to warn other traffic
- ask drivers to switch off their engines and stop smoking
- arrange for the emergency services to be called immediately with full details of the collision location and any casualties (on a motorway, use the emergency telephone which allows easy location by the emergency services. If you use a mobile phone, first make sure you have identified your location from the marker posts on the side of the hard shoulder)
- move uninjured people away from the vehicles to safety; on a motorway this should, if possible, be well away from the traffic, the hard shoulder and the central reservation
- do not move injured people from their vehicles unless they are in immediate danger from fire or explosion
- do not remove a motorcyclist's helmet unless it is essential to do so
- be prepared to give first aid as shown on pages 92 – 93
- stay at the scene until emergency services arrive.

If you are involved in any other medical emergency on the motorway you should contact the emergency services in the same way.

## Collisions involving dangerous goods

**258.** Vehicles carrying dangerous goods are required to display rectangular orange coloured panels to the front and rear. If the vehicle is a road tanker, similar panels are required on both sides and in addition, the UN number for the dangerous goods, the emergency action code and appropriate warning signs must be displayed at the rear.
(see page 82).

**259.** If a collision involves a vehicle containing dangerous goods, follow the advice in Rule 257 and, in particular
- switch off engines and **DO NOT SMOKE**
- keep well away from the vehicle and do not be tempted to

try to rescue casualties as you yourself could become one
- call the emergency services and give as much information as possible about the labels and markings on the vehicle.
**DO NOT** use a mobile phone close to a vehicle carrying inflammable loads.

## Documentation

**260.** If you are involved in a collision which causes damage or injury to any other person, vehicle, animal or property, you **MUST**
- stop
- give your own and the vehicle owner's name and address, and the registration number of the vehicle, to anyone having reasonable grounds for requiring them
- if you do not give your name and address at the time of the collision, report the collision to the police immediately.

*Law RTO 1981 Arts 175 & 176*

**261.** If another person is injured and you do not produce your insurance certificate at the time of the collision to a police officer or to anyone having reasonable grounds to request it, you **MUST**
- report the collision to the police immediately
- produce your insurance certificate for the police as soon as reasonably practicable.

*Law RTO 1981 Art 175*

# Road works

**262.** When the 'Road Works Ahead' sign is displayed, you will need to be more watchful and look for additional signs providing more specific instructions.

- You **MUST NOT** exceed any temporary maximum speed limit.
- Use your mirrors and get into the correct lane for your vehicle in good time and as signs direct.
- Do not switch lanes to overtake queuing traffic.
- Do not drive through an area marked off by traffic cones.
- Watch out for traffic entering or leaving the works area, but do not be distracted by what is going on there.
- Bear in mind that the road ahead may be obstructed by the works or by slow moving or stationary traffic.

*Law RTRO Art 43*

## Additional rules for high speed roads

**263.** Take special care on motorways and other high speed dual carriageways.

- One or more lanes may be closed to traffic and a lower speed limit may apply.
- Works vehicles that are slow moving or stationary with a large 'Keep Left' or 'Keep Right' sign on the back are sometimes used to close lanes for repairs.
- Check mirrors, slow down and change lanes if necessary.
- Keep a safe distance from the vehicle in front (see Rule 105).

**264. Contraflow systems** mean that you may be travelling in a narrower lane than normal and with no permanent barrier between you and oncoming traffic. The hard shoulder may be used for traffic but be aware that there may be broken down vehicles ahead of you. Keep a good distance from the vehicle ahead and observe any temporary speed limits.

# Railway level crossings

**265.** A level crossing is where a road crosses a railway line. Approach and cross it with care. Never drive on to a crossing until the road is clear on the other side and do not get too close to the car in front. Never stop or park on, or near, a crossing.

## Controlled crossings

**266.** Most crossings have traffic light signals with a steady amber light, twin flashing red stop lights (see pages 70 and 75) and an audible alarm for pedestrians. They may have full, half or no barriers.

- You **MUST** always obey the flashing red stop lights.
- You **MUST** stop behind the white line across the road.
- Keep going if you have already crossed the white line when the amber light comes on.
- You **MUST** wait if a train goes by and the red lights continue to flash. This means another train will be passing soon.
- Only cross when the lights go off, audible alarm ceases and barriers open.
- Never zigzag around half-barriers; they lower automatically because a train is approaching.
- At crossings where there are no barriers, a train is close when the lights show.

*Laws RTO 1995 Art 49 & TSR reg 8*

Stop when the traffic lights show

**267. Railway telephones.** If you are driving a large or slow-moving vehicle, or herding animals, a train could arrive before you are clear of the crossing. You **MUST** obey any sign instructing you to use the railway telephone to obtain permission to cross. You **MUST** also telephone when clear of the crossing.

*Laws RTO 1995 Art 49 & TSR reg 8*

**268. Crossings without traffic lights.** You should stop and wait at the barrier or gate when it begins to close and not cross until the barrier or gate opens.

## User-operated gates or barriers
**269.** Some crossings have 'Stop' signs and small red and green lights. You **MUST NOT** cross when the red light is showing; only cross if the green light is on. If crossing with a vehicle, you should
- open the gates or barriers on both sides of the crossing
- check that the green light is still on and cross quickly
- close the gates or barriers when you are clear of the crossing.

*Laws  RTO 1995 Art 49 & TSR reg 8*

**270.** If there are no lights, follow the procedure in Rule 269. Stop, look both ways and listen before you cross. If there is a railway telephone, always use it to contact the signal operator to make sure it is safe to cross. Inform the signal operator again when you are clear of the crossing.

## Open crossings
**271.** These have no gates, barriers, attendant or traffic lights but will have a 'Give Way' sign. You should look both ways, listen and make sure there is no train coming before you cross.

## Collisions and breakdowns
**272.** If your vehicle breaks down, or if you have a collision on a crossing you should
- get everyone out of the vehicle and clear of the crossing immediately
- use a railway telephone if available to tell the signal operator. Follow the instructions you are given
- move the vehicle clear of the crossing if there is time before a train arrives. If the alarm sounds, or the amber light comes on, leave the vehicle and get clear of the crossing immediately.

# Tramways

(Currently applies to Great Britain only. Legislative references relate to Great Britain legislation).

**273.** You **MUST NOT** enter a road, lane or other route reserved for trams. Take extra care where trams run along the road. The width taken up by trams is often shown by tram lanes marked by white lines, yellow dots or by a different type of road surface. Diamond-shaped signs give instructions to tram drivers only.
*Law RTRA sects 5 & 8*

**274.** Take extra care where the track crosses from one side of the road to the other and where the road narrows and the tracks come close to the kerb. Tram drivers usually have their own traffic signals and may be permitted to move when you are not. Always give way to trams. Do not try to race or overtake them.

**275.** You **MUST NOT** park your vehicle where it would get in the way of trams or where it would force other drivers to do so.
*Law RTRA sects 5 & 8*

**276. Tram stops.** Where the tram stops at a platform, either in the middle or at the side of the road, you **MUST** follow the route shown by the road signs and markings. At stops without platforms you **MUST NOT** drive between a tram and the left-hand kerb when a tram has stopped to pick up passengers.
*Law RTRA sects 5 & 8*

**277.** Look out for pedestrians, especially children, running to catch a tram approaching a stop.

**278.** Cyclists and motorcyclists should take extra care when riding close to or crossing the tracks, especially if the rails are wet. It is safest to cross the tracks directly at right angles.

# Light signals controlling traffic

## Traffic Light Signals

RED means 'Stop'. Wait behind the stop line on the carriageway

RED AND AMBER also means 'Stop'. Do not pass through or start until GREEN shows

GREEN means you may go on if the way is clear. Take special care if you intend to turn left or right and give way to pedestrians who are crossing

AMBER means 'Stop' at the stop line. You may go on only if the AMBER appears after you have crossed the stop line or are so close to it that to pull up might cause an accident

A GREEN ARROW may be provided in addition to the full green signal if movement in a certain direction is allowed before or after the full green phase. If the way is clear you may go but only in the direction shown by the arrow. You may do this whatever other lights may be showing. White light signals may be provided for trams

## Flashing red lights

### Alternately flashing red lights mean YOU MUST STOP

At level crossings, lifting bridges, airfields, fire stations, etc

## Motorway signals

Do not proceed further in this lane

Change lane

Reduced visibility ahead

Lane ahead closed

Temporary maximum speed limit and information message

Leave motorway at next exit

Temporary maximum speed limit

End of restriction

## Lane control signals

Green arrow – lane available to traffic facing the sign.
Red crosses – lane closed to traffic facing the sign.
White diagonal arrow – change lanes in direction shown

# Signals to other road users

## Direction indicator signals

I intend to move out to the right or turn right

I intend to move in to the left or turn left or stop on the left

## Brake light signals

I am applying the brakes

## Reversing light signals

I intend to reverse

**These signals should not be used except for the purposes described.**

## Arm signals

For use when direction indicator signals are not used, or when necessary to reinforce direction indicator signals and stop lights. *Also for use by pedal cyclists and those in charge of horses.*

I intend to move in to the left or turn left

I intend to move out to the right or turn right

I intend to slow down or stop

# Signals by authorised persons

## Stop

Traffic approaching
from the front

Traffic approaching from
both front and behind

Traffic approaching
from behind

## To beckon traffic on

From the side

From the front

From behind

## Arm signals to persons controlling traffic

I want to go straight on

I want to turn left;
use either hand

I want to turn right

# Traffic signs

## Signs giving orders
**Signs with red circles are mostly prohibitive.**
**Plates below signs qualify their message.**

Entry to
20 mph zone

End of
20 mph zone

School crossing
patrol

Maximum speed

National speed
limit applies

Stop and
give way

Give way to
traffic on
major road

No vehicles
except bicycles
being pushed

No entry for
vehicular traffic

No right turn

No left turn

No U-turns

Give priority to
vehicles from
opposite
direction

No
overtaking

No motor
vehicles

Manually operated temporary
STOP and GO signs

No buses
(over 8
passenger
seats)

No cycling

No
towed caravans

No vehicles
carrying explosives

No vehicle or
combination of
vehicles over
length shown

No vehicles over
height shown

No vehicles over
width shown

No vehicles over
maximum gross
weight shown
(in tonnes)

No goods vehicles
over maximum
gross weight
shown (in tonnes)
except for loading
and unloading

No waiting

Parking restricted
to permit holders

No stopping
(Clearway)

No stopping during
times shown except
for as long as
necessary to set
down or pick up
passengers

---

Note: Although *The Highway Code* shows many of the signs commonly in use, a comprehensive
explanation of our signing system is given in the booklet *Know Your Traffic Signs*, which is on sale at
booksellers. The booklet also illustrates and explains the vast
majority of signs the road user is likely to encounter. The signs illustrated in *The Highway Code* are
not all drawn to the same scale. Some older designs of signs may still be seen on the roads.

73

**Signs with blue circles but no red border mostly give positive instruction.**

One-way traffic (note: compare circular 'Ahead only' sign)

Ahead only

Turn left ahead (right if symbol reversed)

Turn left (right if symbol reversed)

Keep left (right if symbol reversed)

Route to be used by pedal cycles only

Segregated pedal cycle and pedestrian route

Minimum speed

End of minimum speed

Mini-roundabout (roundabout circulation – give way to vehicles from the immediate right)

Vehicles may pass either side to reach same destination

Buses and cycles only

Trams only

Pedestrian crossing point over tramway

With-flow bus and cycle lane

Contra-flow bus lane

With-flow pedal cycle lane

# Warning signs Mostly triangular

Distance to 'STOP' line ahead

Crossroads

Junction on bend ahead

T-junction

Staggered junction

Distance to 'Give Way' line ahead

**The priority through route is indicated by the broader line.**

Sharp deviation of route to left (or right if chevrons reversed)

Double bend first to left (symbol may be reversed)

Bend to right (or left if symbol reversed)

Roundabout

Uneven road

Plate below some signs

Dual carriage-way ends

Road narrows on right (left if symbol reversed)

Road narrows on both sides

Two-way traffic crosses one-way road

Two-way traffic straight ahead

Traffic signals

Traffic signals not in use

Slippery road

Steep hill downwards

Steep hill upwards

Gradients may be shown as a ratio i.e. 20% = 1:5

# Warning signs – continued

School crossing patrol ahead (some signs have amber lights which flash when children are crossing)

Frail elderly people (or blind or disabled as shown) crossing road

Pedestrians in road ahead

Pedestrian crossing

Traffic queues likely ahead

Cycle route ahead

Side winds

Hump bridge

Worded warning sign

Risk of ice

Risk of grounding

Light signals ahead at level crossing, airfield or bridge

Level crossing with barrier or gate ahead

Level crossing without barrier or gate ahead

Level crossing without barrier

Trams crossing ahead

Cattle

Wild animals

Wild horses or ponies

Accompanied horses or ponies

Quayside or river bank

Opening or swing bridge ahead

Low-flying aircraft or sudden aircraft noise

Falling or fallen rocks

Available width of headroom indicated

Overhead electric cable; plate indicates maximum height of vehicles which can pass safely

Tunnel ahead

Distance over which road humps extend

Other danger; plate indicates nature of danger

Soft verges

# DIrection signs Mostly rectangular
## Signs on motorways – blue backgrounds

At a junction leading directly
into a motorway
(junction number may be shown
on a black background)

On approaches to junctions
(junction number on black
background)

Route confirmatory sign
after junction

Downward pointing arrows mean 'Get in lane'
The left-hand lanes leads to a different destination from the other lanes.

The panel with the inclined arrow indicates the destinations which can be reached
by leaving the motorway at the next junction

## Signs on primary routes – green backgrounds

On approaches to junctions

On approaches to junctions

Motorways shown in brackets can be reached along the route indicated.
White panels indicate local or non-primary routes leading from the junction ahead.
Brown panels show the route to tourist attractions.
The name of the junction may be shown at the top of the sign.
A symbol may be included to warn of a hazard or restriction along that route.

Route confirmatory sign
after junction

At the junction

On approach to a junction

## Signs on non-primary and local routes – black borders

On approaches to junctions

Green panels indicate that the primary route starts at the junction ahead.
Route numbers on a blue background show the direction to a motorway.
Route numbers on a green background show the direction to a primary route.

At the junction

Direction to toilets with access for the disabled

## Other direction signs

Picnic site

National Trust Property

Direction to camping and caravan site

Advisory route for lorries

Tourist attraction

Route for pedal cycles forming part of a National Cycle Network

Route for pedestrians

Diversion route

Recommended route for pedal cycles to place shown

Symbols showing emergency diversion route for motorway and other main road traffic

Direction to a car park

# Information signs All rectangular

Start of motorway and point from which motorway regulations apply

Area in which cameras are used to enforce traffic regulations

Traffic has priority over oncoming vehicles

No through road for vehicles

Hospital ahead with Accident and Emergency facilities

End of motorway

Parking place for solo motorcycles

Advance warning of prohibition ahead

Motorway service area sign showing the operator's name

Tourist information point

Recommended route for pedal cycles

Appropriate traffic lanes at junction ahead

'Countdown' markers at exit from motorway (each bar represents 100 yards to the exit). Green-backed markers may be used on primary routes and white-backed markers with black bars on other routes. At approaches to concealed level crossings white-backed markers with red bars may be used. Although these will be erected at equal distances the bars do not represent 100 yard intervals.

Entrance to controlled parking zone

End of controlled parking zone

With-flow bus lane ahead

Bus lane on road at junction ahead

# Road works signs

Road works

Loose chippings

Road works
1 mile ahead

End of road works
and any temporary
restrictions

Temporary hazard
at road works

Temporary lane closure
(the number and position
of arrows and red bars
may be varied according
to lanes open and closed)

Lane restrictions at
road works ahead

One lane crossover
at contraflow
road works

Signs used on the back of slow-moving or
stationary vehicles warning of a lane closed
ahead by a works vehicle. There are no cones
on the road.

Slow-moving or stationary
works vehicle blocking a traffic
lane. Pass in the direction
shown by the arrow.

Mandatory speed
limit ahead

# Road markings   Across the carriageway

Stop line at signals or
police control

Stop line at 'Stop' sign

Stop line for pedestrians
at a level crossing

Give way to traffic on major road

Give way to traffic from the right
at a roundabout

Give way to traffic from the right
at a mini-roundabout

## Along the carriageway

Edge line

Centre line
See Rule
106

Hazard
warning line
See Rule 106

Double white lines
with reflective studs
See Rules 107 and 108

Diagonal hatching
See Rule 109

Lane line
See Rule
110

# Along the edge of the carriageway

## Waiting restrictions

Waiting restrictions indicated by yellow lines apply to the carriageway, pavement and verge. You may stop to load and unload or while passengers board or alight unless there are also loading restrictions as described below. The times at which the restrictions apply are shown on nearby plates or on entry signs to controlled parking zones. If no days are shown on the signs, the restrictions are in force every day including Sundays and Bank Holidays. White bay markings and upright signs (see below) indicate where parking is allowed. Always check the times shown on the plates.

YELLOW LINES CAN ONLY GIVE A GUIDE TO THE RESTRICTIONS AND CONTROLS IN FORCE AND SIGNS, NEARBY OR AT A ZONE ENTRY, MUST BE CONSULTED.

No waiting
at any time

No waiting
during times
shown on sign

Waiting is limited to the times
and duration shown

# On the kerb or at the edge of the carriageway

## Loading restrictions on roads

Yellow marks on the kerb or at the edge of the carriageway indicate that loading or unloading is prohibited at the times shown on the nearby black and white plates. If no days are indicated on the signs the restrictions are in force every day including Sundays and Bank Holidays.

ALWAYS CHECK THE TIMES SHOWN ON THE PLATES.

Lengths of road reserved for vehicles loading and unloading are indicated by a white 'bay' marking with the words 'Loading Only' and a sign with the white on blue 'trolley' symbol. This sign also shows whether loading and unloading is restricted to goods vehicles and the times at which the bay can be used. If no times or days are shown it may be used at any time. Vehicles may not park here if they are not loading or unloading.

No loading or unloading at any time

No loading or unloading at the times shown

Loading bay

# Other road markings

Keep entrance clear of stationary vehicles, even if picking up or setting down children

Warning of 'Give Way' just ahead

Parking space reserved for vehicles named

See Rule 217

See Rule 120

Box junction See Rule 150

Do not block entrance to side road

Indication of traffic lanes

# Vehicle markings

## Large goods vehicle rear markings

Motor vehicles over 7500 kilograms maximum gross weight and trailers over 3500 kilograms maximum gross weight

Rear markings prescribed for motor vehicles and trailers whenever first used or manufactured

Permitted markings for vehicles first used before 24 January 1996 and trailers manufactured before 24 January 1996.

The vertical markings are also required to be fitted to builders' skips placed in the road.

School bus
(displayed
front or rear
of bus
or coach)

## Hazard warning plates

Certain tank vehicles carrying dangerous goods
must display hazard information panels

The above panel will be
displayed by vehicles
carrying certain
dangerous goods

**2YE**
**1089**
FLAMMABLE LIQUID
3
Newtown-on-Moors
**(0123) 45678**

The panel illustrated may be displayed to indicate
the carriage of hazardous goods.

Diamond symbols indicating other risks include:

Toxic substance    Non-flammable    Spontaneously    Corrosive
6                  compressed        combustible      substance
                   gas               substance        8
TOXIC              2                 4
        Oxidizing          Radioactive
        substance          substance
        5.1                7

## Projection markers

Side marker

End marker

Both required when load or equipment
(eg crane jib) overhangs front or rear by
more than two metres

# Annexes

## 1. Choosing and maintaining your bicycle

Make sure that

- you choose the right size of cycle for comfort and safety
- lights and reflectors are kept clean and in good working
  order
- tyres are in good condition and inflated to the pressure
  shown on the tyre
- gears are working correctly
- the chain is properly adjusted and oiled
- the saddle and handlebars are adjusted to the correct
  height.

You **MUST**

- ensure your brakes are efficient
- ensure a working bell or horn is fitted
- between sunset and sunrise, use lit front and rear lights and
  display an efficient red rear reflector.

*Laws RV(T)R reg 7, RVLR reg 21*

# 2. Motorcycle licence requirements

**If you have a provisional motorcycle licence or a full car licence** you may ride motorcycles up to 125cc and 11kW power output, with L plates on public roads.

**If you have a full moped licence** and wish to obtain full motorcycle entitlement you will be required to take a motorcycle theory test if you did not take a separate theory test when you obtained your moped licence. You **MUST** then pass a practical motorcycle test.

*Law MV (DL)R reg 31 (1)*

**Light motorcycle licence (A1):** you take a test on a motorcycle of between 75 and 120cc. If you pass you may ride a motorcycle up to 125cc with power output up to 11kW.

**Standard motorcycle licence (A):** if your test vehicle is between 120 and 125cc and capable of more than 100 kph you will be given a standard (A) licence. You will then be restricted to motorcycles of up to 25 kW for two years, not counting any periods of disqualification or revocation. After two years you may ride any size of machine.

You **MUST NOT** carry a pillion passenger or pull a trailer until you have passed your test.

*Law MV(DL)R reg 12*

## Moped licence requirements

Mopeds are up to 50cc with a maximum speed of 50 kph.

**To ride a moped,** learners **MUST**
• be 16 or over
• have a provisional moped licence
You **MUST** first pass the theory test for motorcycles and then the moped practical test to obtain your full moped licence.

If you have a full car licence or motorcycle licence you are qualified to ride a moped without L plates.

**Note.** The following gives exemption from taking the theory test
• full car licence
• full A1 motorcycle licence gained after 1/1/97
• full moped licence gained after 1/7/97.

*Law MV(DL)R*

# 3. Motor vehicle documentation, learner and restricted driver requirements

## Documents

**Driving Licence.** You **MUST** have a valid signed driving licence for the category of vehicle you are driving. You **MUST** inform Driver and Vehicle Licensing Northern Ireland (DVLNI) if you change your name and address.
*Law RTO 1981 Art 3*

**Insurance.** You **MUST** have a valid insurance certificate covering you for third party liability. Before driving any vehicle, make sure that it has this cover for your use or that your own insurance gives you adequate cover. You **MUST NOT** drive a vehicle without insurance.
*Law RTO 1981 Art 90*

**MOT.** Cars and motorcycles **MUST** normally pass an MOT test four years from the date of the first registration and every year after that. You **MUST NOT** drive a vehicle without an MOT certificate, when it should have one. Driving an unroadworthy vehicle may invalidate your insurance. Exceptionally you may drive to a pre-arranged test appointment or to a garage for repairs required for the test.
*Law RTO 1995 Arts 61, 63, 65 & 69*

**Vehicle Registration Document.** Registration documents are issued for all motor vehicles used on the road, describing them (make, model, etc.) and giving details of the registered keeper. You **MUST** notify Driver and Vehicle Licensing Northern Ireland (DVLNI) in Coleraine as soon as possible when you buy or sell a vehicle, or if you change your name or address.
*Law RV(R&L)R Arts 11, 13 & 14*

**Statutory Off The Road Notification (SORN)** Where a registered keeper is not renewing a vehicle licence because the vehicle is being taken off the road, they must notify Driver and Vehicle Licensing (DVLNI) and make a declaration that the vehicle is off the road. This is known as a SORN declaration.
*Law RV (R&L)R Art 26*

**Vehicle Excise Duty.** All vehicles used or kept on the roads **MUST** have a valid Vehicle Excise Duty disc (tax disc) displayed at all times. Any vehicle exempt from duty **MUST** display a nil licence.
*Law VERA sect 29*

**Production of documents.** You **MUST** be able to produce your driving licence and counterpart, a valid insurance certificate and (if appropriate) a valid MOT certificate, when requested by a police officer. If you cannot do this you may be asked to take them to a police station within seven days.
*Law RTO 1981 Art 180*

## Learner drivers
Learners driving a car **MUST** hold a valid provisional licence. They **MUST** be supervised by someone at least 21 years old who holds a full EC/EEA licence for that type of car (automatic or manual) and has held one for at least three years.
*Law MV(DL)R reg 12*

**Vehicles.** Any vehicle driven by a learner **MUST** display red L plates. Plates **MUST** conform to legal specifications and **MUST** be clearly visible to others from in front of the vehicle and from behind. Plates should be removed or covered when not being driven by a learner.
The maximum speed limit for vehicles displaying L plates is 45mph, except goods vehicles, buses and coaches on a motorway.
*Laws MV(DL)R reg 12, RTO 1981 Art 19, MV(SLRE)R reg 2*

You **MUST** pass the theory test (if one is required) and then a practical driving test for the category of vehicle you wish to drive before driving unaccompanied.
*Law MV(DL)R reg 30*

## Restricted drivers
After passing the driving test for a motor car or motorcycle, you must display amber R plates for a period of one year from the date of passing the test. The plates **MUST** conform to legal specifications and **MUST** be clearly visible to others from in front of the vehicle and from behind. Plates should be removed or covered when not being driven by a restricted driver. The maximum permitted speed for any vehicle displaying R plates is 45mph, irrespective of whether or not the vehicle is being driven by a restricted driver.
*Laws RTO 1981 Art 19A & MV(PR)R*

# 4. The road user and the law

## Road traffic law

The following list can be found abbreviated throughout the Code. It is not intended to be a comprehensive guide, but a guide to some of the important points of law. For the precise wording of the law, please refer to the various Orders, Acts and Regulations (as amended) indicated in the Code. Abbreviations are listed below.

Most of the provisions apply on all roads throughout Northern Ireland. A road is a 'public road (including bridges or tunnels over which a public road passes) and any street, carriageway, highway or roadway to which the public has access'. It is important to note that references to 'road' therefore generally include footpaths and cycle tracks and many roadways and driveways on private land (including many car parks). In most cases, the law will apply to them and there may be additional rules for particular paths or ways. Some serious driving offences, including drink-driving offences, also apply to all public places, for example public car parks.

| | |
|---|---|
| Motor Vehicles (Construction & Use) Regulations (NI) 1999 | CUR |
| Horses (Protective Headgear for Young Riders) (NI) Order 1990 | H(PHYR)0 |
| Horses (Protective Headgear for Young Riders) Regulations (NI) 1992 | H(PHYR)R |
| Motor Cars (Driving Instruction)(Amendment) Regulations (NI) 2002 | MC(DI)(A)R |
| Motor Cycles (Eye Protectors) Regulations (NI) 2000 | MC(EP)R |
| Motor Cycles (Protective Headgear) Regulations (NI) 1999 | MC(PH)R |
| Motor Vehicles (Driving Licences) Regulations (NI) 1996 | MV(DL)R |
| Motor Vehicles Driving Licences (Amendment) Regulations (NI) 2002 | MVDL(A) |
| Motor Vehicles (Prescribed Restrictions) Regulations (NI) 1996 | MV(PR)R |
| Motor Vehicles (Speed Limits) Regulations (NI) 1989 | MV(SL)R |
| Motor Vehicles (Speed Limit Restriction) (Exemption) Regulations (NI) 1998 | MV(SLRE)R |
| Motor Vehicles (Wearing of Seat Belts) Regulations (NI) 1993 | MV(WSB)R |
| Motor Vehicles (Wearing Seat Belts by Children in Front Seats) Regulations (NI) 1993 | MV(WSBBCFS)R |
| Motorways Traffic Regulations (NI) 1984 | MTR |
| 'Pelican' Pedestrian Crossing Regulations (NI) 1989 | PPCR |

| | |
|---|---|
| Road Traffic (NI) Order 1981 or 1995 (as indicated) | RTO |
| Road Traffic Offenders (NI) Order 1996 | RTOO |
| Road Traffic Regulation (NI) Order 1997 | RTRO |
| Road Traffic (Traffic Wardens) Order (NI) 1976 | RT(TW)O |
| Road Vehicles Lighting Regulations (NI) 2000 | RVLR |
| Road Vehicles (Registration & Licensing) Regulations (NI) 2002 | RV(R&L)R |
| Road Traffic (New Drivers) (NI) Order 1998 | RT(ND)O |
| Road Vehicles (Traffic) Regulations 1933 | RV(T)R |
| Roads (NI) Order 1993 | RO |
| Roads (Restriction of Waiting) Order (NI) 1982 | R(RW)0 |
| Road Vehicles (Display of Registration Marks) Regulations 2001 | RV(DRM)R |
| Traffic Signs Regulations (NI) 1997 | TSR |
| Vehicle Excise and Registration Act 1994 | VERA |
| 'Zebra' Pedestrian Crossings Regulations (NI) 1974 | ZPCR |

# 5. Penalties

Parliament has set the maximum penalties for road traffic offences. The seriousness of the offence is reflected in the maximum penalty. It is for the courts to decide what sentence to impose according to circumstances.

The penalty table on page 88 indicates some of the main offences and the associated penalties. There is a wide range of other more specific offences which, for the sake of simplicity, are not shown here.

The penalty points and disqualification system is described below.

## Penalty points and disqualification

The penalty point system is intended to deter drivers from following unsafe driving practices. The court MUST order points to be endorsed on the licence according to the fixed number or the range set by Parliament. The accumulation of penalty points acts as a warning to drivers that they risk disqualification if further offences are committed.

A driver who accumulates 12 or more penalty points within a three year period must be disqualified. This will be for a minimum period of six months, or longer if the driver has previously been disqualified.

For every offence which carries penalty points the court has a discretionary power to order the licence holder to be disqualified. This may be for any period the court thinks fit, but will usually be between a week and a few months.

# Penalty table

Offence · Maximum penalties

| Offence | IMPRISONMENT | FINE | DISQUALIFICATION | PENALTY POINTS |
|---|---|---|---|---|
| *Causing death, or grievous bodily injury, by dangerous driving | 10 years | Unlimited | Obligatory–2 years minimum | 3–11 (if exceptionally not disqualified) |
| *Dangerous driving | 2 years | Unlimited | Obligatory | 3–11 (if exceptionally not disqualified) |
| *Causing death, or grievous bodily injury by careless driving when under the influence of drink or drugs | 10 years | Unlimited | Obligatory–2 years minimum | 3–11 (if exceptionally not disqualified) |
| Careless or inconsiderate driving | - | £2,500 | Discretionary | 3–9 |
| **Driving while unfit through drink or drugs or with excess alcohol; or failing to provide a specimen for analysis | 6 months | £5,000 | Obligatory | 3–11 (if exceptionally not disqualified) |
| Failing to stop after an accident or failing to report an accident | 6 months | £5,000 | Discretionary | 5–10 |
| Driving when disqualified | 1 year | Unlimited | Discretionary | 6 |
| Driving without insurance | - | £5,000 | Discretionary | 6–8 |
| Driving without a licence | - | £1,000 | Discretionary | 3–6 |
| Speeding | - | £1,000 | Discretionary | 3–6 or 3 (fixed penalty) |
| Traffic light offences | - | £1,000 | Discretionary | 3 |
| No MOT certificate | - | £1,000 | - | - |
| Seat belt offences | - | £500 | - | - |
| Dangerous cycling | - | £2,500 | - | - |
| Careless cycling | - | £1,000 | - | - |
| Failing to identify driver of a vehicle | - | £1,000 | Discretionary | 3 |

* Where a court disqualifies a person on conviction for one of these offences, it must order an extended retest and for those offences marked
* *it must order an ordinary retest.
The courts also have discretion to order a retest for any other offence which carries penalty points: an extended test following a penalty points disqualification and an ordinary test in any other case.

In the case of serious offences, such as dangerous driving and drink-driving, the court **MUST** order disqualification. The minimum period is 12 months, but for repeat offenders or where the alcohol level is high, it may be longer. For example, a second drink-drive offence in the space of 10 years will result in a minimum of three years' disqualification.

Furthermore, in some serious cases, the court **MUST** (in addition to imposing a fixed period of disqualification) order the offender to be disqualified until they pass a driving test. In other cases the court has a discretionary power to order such disqualification. The test may be an ordinary length test or an extended test according to the nature of the offence.
*Laws RTOO Arts 30, 31, 35, 40 & 41*

**New drivers.** Special rules apply to drivers within two years of the date of passing their driving test if they passed the test after 14 December 1998 and held nothing but a provisional (learner) licence before passing the test. If the number of penalty points on their licence reaches six or more as a result of offences they commit before the two years are over (including any they committed before they passed the test), their licence will be revoked. They must then reapply for a provisional licence and may drive only as learners until they pass a theory and practical driving test.
*RT(ND)O*

**Note.** This applies even if they pay by fixed penalty. Drivers who already have a full licence for one type of vehicle are not affected by this when they pass a test to drive another type.

## Other consequences of offending
Where an offence is committed under a Road Traffic Order, the vehicle used to commit the offence may be subject to forfeiture.

In addition to the penalties a court may decide to impose, the cost of insurance is likely to rise considerably following conviction for a serious driving offence. This is because insurance companies consider such drivers are more likely to have a collision.

Drivers convicted of drinking and driving twice within 10 years, or once if they are over two and a half times the legal limit, or those who refused to give a specimen, also have to satisfy Driver and Vehicle Licensing Northern Ireland's Medical Branch that they do not have an alcohol problem and are otherwise fit to drive before their licence is returned at the end of their period of disqualification. Persistent misuse of drugs or alcohol may lead to the withdrawal of a driving licence.

# 6. Vehicle maintenance, safety and security

## Vehicle maintenance

Take special care that lights, brakes, steering, exhaust system, seat belts, demisters, wipers and washers are all working. Also

- lights, indicators, reflectors and number plates **MUST** be kept clean and clear
- windscreens and windows **MUST** be kept clean and free from obstructions to vision
- lights **MUST** be properly adjusted to prevent dazzling other road users. Extra attention needs to be paid to this if the vehicle is heavily loaded
- exhaust emissions **MUST NOT** exceed prescribed levels
- ensure your seat, seat belt, head restraint and mirrors are adjusted correctly before you drive
- items of luggage are securely stowed.

*Law: many regulations within CUR cover the above equipment and RVLR regs 26 & 29*


### *Warning displays*

Make sure that you understand the meaning of all warning displays on the vehicle instrument panel. Do not ignore warning signs; they could indicate a dangerous fault developing.

- When you turn the ignition key, warning lights will be illuminated but will go out when the engine starts (except the handbrake warning light). If they do not, or if they come on whilst you are driving, stop and investigate the problem, as you could have a serious fault.
- If the charge warning light comes on while you are driving, it may mean that the battery isn't charging. This must  be checked as soon as possible to avoid loss of power to lights and other electrical systems.


### *Tyres*

Tyres **MUST** be correctly inflated and be free from certain cuts and other defects.

**Cars, light vans and light trailers MUST** have a tread depth

of at least 1.6mm across the central three-quarters of the breadth of the tread and around the entire circumference **Motorcycles, large vehicles and passenger carrying vehicles MUST** have a tread depth of at least 1mm across three-quarters of the breadth of the tread and in a continuous band around the entire circumference.
**Mopeds** should have visible tread.
*Laws CUR reg 25*

If a tyre bursts while you are driving, try to keep control of your vehicle. Grip the steering wheel firmly and allow the vehicle to roll to a stop at the side of the road.

If you have a flat tyre, stop as soon as it is safe to do so. Only change the tyre if you can do so without putting yourself or others at risk – otherwise call a breakdown service.

**Tyre pressures.** Check weekly. Do this before your journey, when tyres are cold. Warm or hot tyres may give a misleading reading.

Your brakes and steering will be adversely affected by under-inflated or over-inflated tyres. Excessive or uneven tyre wear may be caused by faults in the braking or suspension systems, or wheels which are out of alignment. Have these faults corrected as soon as possible.

### Fluid levels
Check the fluid levels in your vehicle at least weekly. Low brake fluid may result in brake failure and an accident. Make sure you recognise the low fluid warning lights if your vehicle has them fitted.

### Before winter
Ensure that the battery is well maintained and that there are appropriate anti-freeze agents in your radiator and windscreen bottle.

### Other problems
If your vehicle
- pulls to one side when braking, it is most likely to be a brake fault or incorrectly inflated tyres. Consult a garage or mechanic immediately
- continues to bounce after pushing down on the front or rear, its shock absorbers are worn. Worn shock absorbers

can seriously affect the operation of a vehicle and should be replaced
- smells of anything unusual such as burning rubber, petrol or electrical, investigate immediately. Do not risk a fire.

### Overheated engines or fire
Most engines are water cooled. If your engine overheats you should wait until it has cooled naturally. Only then remove the coolant filler cap and add water or other coolant.

If your vehicle catches fire, get the occupants out of the vehicle quickly and to a safe place. Do not attempt to extinguish a fire in the engine compartment, as opening the bonnet will make the fire flare. Call the fire brigade.

### Petrol stations
Never smoke or use a mobile phone on the forecourt of petrol stations as this is a major fire risk and could cause an explosion.

## Vehicle security
**When you leave your vehicle** you should
- remove the ignition key and engage the steering lock
- lock the car, even if you only leave it for a few minutes
- close the windows completely
- never leave children or pets in an unventilated car
- take all contents with you, or lock them in the boot. Remember, for all a thief knows a carrier bag may contain valuables. Never leave vehicle documents in the car.

**For extra security** fit an anti-theft device such as an alarm or immobiliser. If you are buying a new car it is a good idea to check the level of built-in security features. Consider having your registration number etched on all your car windows. This is a cheap and effective deterrent to professional thieves.

## 7. First aid on the road
In the event of a collision, you can do a number of things to help, even if you have had no training.

### 1. Deal with danger
Further collisions and fire are the main dangers following a collision. Approach any vehicle involved with care. Switch off all engines and, if possible, warn other traffic. Stop anyone from smoking.

## 2. Get help

Try to get the assistance of bystanders. Get someone to call the appropriate emergency services as soon as possible. They will need to know the exact location of the collision and the number of vehicles involved.

## 3. Help those involved

**DO NOT** move casualties still in vehicles unless further danger is threatened. **DO NOT** remove a motorcyclist's helmet unless it is essential. **DO NOT** give the casualty anything to eat or drink. **DO** try to make them comfortable and prevent them from getting cold, but avoid unnecessary movement. **DO** give reassurance confidently to the casualty. They may be shocked but prompt treatment will minimise this.

## 4. Provide emergency care

Follow the *ABC of First aid*

**A** is for **Airway** – check for and relieve any obstruction to breathing. Remove any obvious obstruction in the mouth. Breathing may begin and colour improve.

**B** is for **Breathing** – if breathing does not begin when the airway has been cleared, lift the chin and tilt the head very gently backwards. Pinch the casualty's nostrils and blow into the mouth until the chest rises; withdraw, then repeat regularly once every four seconds until the casualty can breathe unaided.

**C** is for **Circulation** – prevent blood loss to maintain circulation. If bleeding is present apply firm hand pressure over the wound, preferably using some clean material, without pressing on any foreign body in the wound. Secure a pad with a bandage or length of cloth. Raise the limb to lessen the bleeding, provided it is not broken.

Always carry a first aid kit. You could save a life by learning emergency aid and first aid from a qualified organisation, such as the local ambulance services, the St John Ambulance Association and Brigade, the Order of Malta Ambulance Corps, the British Red Cross or any suitable qualified body.

# Appendix

## Roundabouts are safe and simple

**If you know and use these rules…**

*Many drivers are satisfied with their own use of roundabouts, but believe others do it all wrong! Before criticising other drivers' roundabout behaviour, check your own knowledge of the rules.*

### Why roundabouts?

Used properly, roundabouts smooth traffic flow at busy junctions. Vehicles can enter and leave roundabouts by different roads with less inconvenience or danger. They are really circular, clockwise, one-way traffic systems enabling several traffic streams to mix.

### The rules for using roundabouts

**Give way:** the most important rule - when entering a roundabout, give way to traffic on the roundabout, unless road markings or signs say otherwise. If the way is clear keep moving. Stopping at a clear roundabout slows traffic and can cause frustrating delays.

A roundabout entrance is usually marked by a single broken line across the road. Sometimes you may find other markings. At some roundabouts one traffic lane might be allowed to flow free; there will be road markings or signs to show this.

**Speed:** approach so that you can stop and give way if necessary. Approaching too fast could make drivers on the roundabout think that you are going to drive in front of them. They could brake or swerve and perhaps cause a collision. If you approach too fast and brake hard at a roundabout entrance you could also cause a collision by panicking a following driver who might skid into the back of your vehicle.

On the roundabout, you should drive according to road, weather and traffic conditions as well as the roadholding qualities of your vehicle.

**Position and Signals:** being correctly positioned and signalling clearly in good time helps other road users. Knowing and following the rules improves traffic flow and safety at roundabouts.

While this appendix provides general advice, other factors such as signs, road markings and the position and type of other vehicles can influence the choice of lane. Where there are signs or road markings, which indicate appropriate lanes, these should assume priority over the following procedures.

**Correct roundabout procedure**

Imagine that you are approaching a busy roundabout with six converging roads. Follow the advice in the diagrams. Treat the roundabout as if it were a clock face. All movement on roundabouts is clockwise.

Always assume that your approach is from the six o'clock position. Approach at the correct speed and in the right gear. Always signal your intentions clearly. If there is no traffic at or on the roundabout you may take the shortest and most convenient route through it. Cancel your signal after leaving the roundabout.

Now that you know the rules, show a good example to other drivers by following them every time. They may even copy your driving style and do it right too!

### 1. Taking the first exit (b) at 8 o'clock

| | |
|---|---|
| **Approach** | Left Lane |
| **Signal** | Left-turn indicator on approach |
| **On Roundabout** | Keep in left lane |
| **Exit** | Keep left-turn indicator going until just after leaving the roundabout. |

## 2. Taking second exit (c) at 10 o'clock

| | |
|---|---|
| **Approach** | Left Lane |
| **Signal** | No approach signal |
| **On Roundabout** | Keep in left lane |
| **Exit** | Use the left-turn indicator when you have passed exit (b) before the one you want to take. |

## 3. Taking third exit (d) at 12 o'clock

| | |
|---|---|
| **Approach** | Left Lane (use right lane if left lane is blocked) |
| **Signal** | No approach signal |
| **On Roundabout** | Keep in left lane (use right lane if approach was in right lane) |
| **Exit** | Use left-turn indicator when you have passed exit (c) before the one you want to take (d). |

### 4. Taking the fourth exit (e) at 2 o'clock

| | |
|---|---|
| **Approach** | Right Lane |
| **Signal** | Right-turn indicator on approach |
| **On Roundabout** | Keep in right lane near centre of roundabout; keep right-turn indicator going |
| **Exit** | Look behind, change to left-turn indicator when you have passed exit (d) before the one you want to take (e). Check behind over your left shoulder and ease into left lane for exit (e). |

### 5. Taking fifth exit (f) at 4 o'clock

| | |
|---|---|
| **Approach** | Right Lane |
| **Signal** | Right-turn indicator on approach |
| **On Roundabout** | Keep in right lane near centre of roundabout; keep right-turn indicator going |
| **Exit** | Look behind, change to left-turn indicator when you have passed exit (e) before the one you want to take (f). Check behind over your left shoulder and ease into left lane for exit (f). |

# Index